M000002544

Life Begins at 60

Life Begins at 60

A New View on Motherhood, Marriage, and Reinventing Ourselves

DR. FRIEDA BIRNBAUM

Skyhorse Publishing

Copyright © 2016 by Frieda Birnbaum

All rights reserved. No part of this book may be reproduced in any manner without the express written consent of the publisher, except in the case of brief excerpts in critical reviews or articles. All inquiries should be address to Skyhorse Publishing, 307 West 36th Street, 11th Floor, New York, NY 10018.

Skyhorse Publishing books may be purchased in bulk at special discounts for sales promotion, corporate gifts, fund-raising, or educational purposes. Special editions can also be created to specifications. For details, contact the Special Sales Department, Skyhorse Publishing, 307 West 36th Street, 11th Floor, New York, NY 10018.

Skyhorse® and Skyhorse Publishing® are registered trademarks or Skyhorse Publishing, Inc.®, a Delaware corporation.

Visit our website at www.skyhorsepublishing.com.

10 9 8 7 6 5 4 3 2 1

Library of Congress Cataloging-in-Publication Data is available on file.

Cover photograph © Domenic Croce
Central insert photographs reprinted with permission.

ISBN: 978-1-5107-0825-9
Ebook ISBN: 978-1-5107-0827-3

Printed in the United States of America

To Jaeson, Alana, Ari, Jaret, and Josh.

CONTENTS

EDITOR'S PREFACE

A FTER GIVING BIRTH TO TWINS JOSH AND JARET through IVF at sixty years old, Frieda Birnbaum became a household name. The doctor who delivered the twins in Hackensack, New Jersey, alerted the media and soon she was being interviewed on a host of daytime talk shows. Right away, the happily married New Jersey therapist dubbed "the grannymom" received a mixed bag of comments from viewers, readers, and people in her community.

Many questioned her decision, calling her "selfish" (and worse). At the same time their curiosity was piqued: was it even possible to give birth that late in life? Journalists described her as "well-coiffed" in her post-birth photo (really, Frieda later confided, she had just taken a toothbrush to her hair in that hospital bed) and whispered about a need for attention; was this lady for real? Was she desperate, for some reality show or just our attention, and did she even know what she was doing? Was this blonde clueless?

Others, less offended by the telegenic "grannymom," were curious: could pregnancy be maneuvered in one's forties and fifty and at ages well beyond sixty? How could others follow in Frieda's footsteps, and if it were as easy as she made it seem, would this change the game for women regarding not just motherhood but also dating, marriage, career, and personal development in general?

Nine years ago, when she became the oldest mother of twins in the entire United States, she wasn't sure how her story would turn out. But now, the answer is surprising her.

Among the main criticisms lobbed at the sixty-year-old Frieda Birnbaum: she would lack the energy that new mothers implicitly have, which all babies deserve. She would be tired. She would be overwhelmed by babies' and then young children's demands, which she would not be able to meet, thus cheating them out of a normal life.

* * *

Frieda is a psychotherapist who sees patients in her home office. The home itself is cavernous and tasteful, with a big backyard. And yes, it's enviable by anyone's standards; these twins, ensconced in leafy Saddle River, New Jersey, live across the street from Wyclef Jean and a stone's throw from other celebrities seeking the ultimate in comfy suburban life. Josh and Jaret have a salamander, a newt, a snake, and a small dog.

Frieda herself is always doing a million things at once. At sixty-nine, she's a surprising mother — but she's not only that. She gets involved, for instance, in local politics. At her synagogue, she gives poignant and animated speeches about her parents and grandparents, who narrowly escaped being murdered in the Holocaust. Quietly confident and a good listener one-on-one, Frieda somewhat paradoxically relishes telling stories for an audience—especially when she thinks she can help them with some aspect of their life, illuminate a part of a shared Jewish past, and open their eyes in some insightful, even motherly, way. It's the same on the radio: several times a week, she calls in to regional broadcasts around the United States. She is asked to comment on whichever events are trending: the Duggars, Hillary Clinton, Bill Cosby and his string of alleged assaults. She is famous for defying the motherhood odds, but she doesn't talk about the that when she's being interviewed on New York's WPIX11 about current events; instead, she's sharing advice as a storyteller, and as a psychoanalyst with decades of experience advising clients on the exact same subject for which she's come under scrutiny: the family dynamic, and how to fine-tune it. How to keep spice in the marriage, or more importantly, how to retain your spouse's respect as years pass. How to be there—to *really* be there—for one's children, and how to advise and support them in today's world, where bullies abound and it is harder and harder to be a kid.

Not everyone has a spare ten thousand or two lying around for egg-freezing, but nonetheless, it's heartening to think that reproductive medicine may be able to offer an alternative to living in fear of a ticking biological clock. And if there is anyone suitable for breaking the mold of motherhood and thoroughly *updating* the world "granny-mom," then it is Frieda Birnbaum. For not only has Frieda raised twins born when she was sixty: she also reinvented her career and breathed new life into her marriage. And if you were to ask her what her proudest achievement has been *since* turning sixty—an age when many New York-area wives start thinking of Miami Beach shuffleboard and water aerobics, with occasional visits from grandchildren—I know how she'd answer. Her mission has been to get out her message, loud and clear: family issues can be overcome, with compassion and the benefit of wise hindsight; the world's biggest issues (on which she's often asked to comment, nowadays), like the pernicious spread ISIS or the question of who our next President will be, can be broken down and understood by contemplating the real people involved; and at the individual level, we should never, ever let anyone tell us "no" in the face of our dreams.

It works out well, on top of all this, that Frieda Birnbaum's most treasured message is one she embodies perfectly: *do not fear growing older.* Unsurpassed energy, the brainpower to embrace a new career, a new view on your husband or wife, or best friend, or yourself . . . a louder, prouder voice . . . a glamorous new look . . . and just plain excitement: you can wake up to all these things any morning, at any age. And as long as you refuse to fear age, then it will only get better and better from here. I have to believe that, anyway. After all, Frieda Birnbaum and her family are living proof.

PART I

MOTHERHOOD AND MORE: MY FAMILY'S STORIES

1

*A Birth Heard
'Round the World*

Eight years ago, when I lay in a hospital bed preparing to give birth, all the major news outlets I could name were enthralled by the idea of reporting it. No wonder: I came with a superlative, a key word ending in "–est": at sixty, I was the oldest woman in America to give birth to twins.

The birth went well, and my husband and I brought the boys home. The weeks that followed were full to the brim as I juggled the elation of holding babies with the chaos of changing two diapers. Amid the newborns' crying fits, giggles, and burps, something familiar replayed on a loop in my brain: people's criticism.

SHOCK AND OUTRAGE

Every phone conversation with my oldest son felt like a screaming match. Offended, as though I had had my twins to spite him, he refused to see his brothers for the first three years of their lives. While I put my boys to bed at night, reading them stories and lying in bed with them till their breathing grew even and I knew they were dreaming, I was also thinking of my other son and wondering how angry he was with me that day.

At a lower volume in my head I would play the voices of my many media critics. During the whirlwind of publicity following my sons' birth, I had been approached by, and then appeared on, a dizzying array of shows including *20/20*, *ABC News*, and *Inside Edition*. There were questions from interviewers and opinions from viewers. "Why would you have a baby at 53, and then twins at sixty? What's wrong with you? You are selfish, crazy, deranged. Why not lavish this energy on *grand*kids? Why not adopt? You've had your turn to give birth, so why insist on doing it now?"

Over and over, I was asked *why* I chose motherhood at sixty years old.

When I claimed independence, saying I made the choice because of a deeply personal desire to give birth at an age many consider to be over the hill, then I was selfish, and implicitly a bad person. After all, they said, I would be in my late seventies when they went to college, and probably become a grandmother to my babies' future babies in my late eighties or even nineties. How could I run after them, help them with homework, volunteer at the school?

I was denying these children of a suitable mother, many said. These critics, mostly women hailing from all over the country and even internationally, seemed to speak not from concern but from a place of anger, tinged with envy, certainly bitter: in short, they seemed to be saying, *How dare she?*

On the other hand, if I admitted being driven to please my husband, or of wanting to provide a younger sibling for my then-youngest son Ari, there was another uproar. I was seen as retrograde, transgressive, a mess of a woman whose needs were being squelched by patriarchal dominance. Or I was a desperate, aging housewife, clinging ridiculously her husband's dwindling approval by putting her body through this unnatural experience, with soon-to-be-neglected twin boys as the unfortunate byproduct.

TV shows, newspapers, and magazines wanted me to explain myself in sound bytes, easily criticized for being either too self-centered or desperately, cluelessly dependent. Regardless of how I responded, people were quick to voice criticisms that pierced the core of who I was as a woman, whether too selfish or too unselfish. I was almost unilaterally resented while my husband, even older than I was and a big proponent of my giving birth at sixty, was spared the venomous critique.

Those who called my giving birth thoughtless or superficial might have been surprised to learn that I'd spent decades studying the impact of career, relationships, and family life on women's happiness; although I couldn't say for sure that doing this would make me beatifically happy, it was safe to say I knew what I was doing and was going into the situation with my eyes wide open. And those who called me selfish would've been surprised to learn that it wasn't just my decision; my husband's desires played a major role. He wanted this, and I internalized his wants just as I had done for my parents, for my children, for friends and foes and colleagues, and even for my in-laws. Like nearly everything I have done in life, giving birth to the twins reflected my volition as well as that of the people around me.

WHEN LABELS DON'T STICK

Labels were thrown my way. Particularly common was "old," which I never thought would be my identifying adjective. While I rested in the hospital, post-birth, one visiting journalist said, "I have come from Germany to see the Old Lady."

"I am the Old Lady," I nodded.

"Really?'" he asked, "You look like you're in your forties."

I smiled at the compliment. But really, it felt odd to be labeled as Old. Because even after giving birth to twins at sixty years old, I didn't feel old at all. In fact, I felt more energized in my life, more excited about the future, than ever before. But was the German journalist right? Was I really the Old Lady?

In the years since that interview, as life went back to normal and I began the real work of raising my sons, I came to know beyond doubt that the label wouldn't stick on me. I was over sixty, true, but deep inside I felt alive, perhaps moreso than ever: yes, life was beginning, not just for my twins but also, in many respects, for me.

In the days and hours leading up to the twins' birth, my hospital clinic almost had to close because of all the calls, some from as far away as Nigeria, Germany, and Poland. My private email account exploded. And typically these messages were not wishing me good luck or saying "get well soon." Instead, people were expressing extreme *concern* for the welfare of my twins.

It all felt surreal. Because even though my pregnancy had made international headlines, my story is not far-fetched–especially compared to that of my mother, who had four children during a long war, with no food and devastation all around. I had healthful meals, hospital care, and a prominent doctor. The twins would go home to a comfortable house, with two loving parents and three older siblings, who would shower them with care and ful-fil every material need. Yet so many were outraged, their focus laser-tight on my perceived irresponsibility. It was all about tearing down the "grannymom."

That label bugged me. Yes, many women become grandmothers, not new mothers, at the age of sixty. I was a "bubby" to my grown-up son Jaeson's young kids, my grandchildren, who lived near us in suburban New Jersey. To my own children, Jaeson, Alana, Ari, and now Josh and Jaret, I was simply a mother.

And anyway, there was something so demeaning about that title. It was like I was being told that was *all* I was. The truth is that even though I love my children infinitely, they do not define me as a person. The same can be said for the many clients I see through private practice, often women who want to be recognized for who they are deep inside. Our identities are who *we* are, not what we do for our children.

After all, those of us who invest too fully in our identities as mothers face a rude awakening when they leave home. We should not lose who we are, through our husbands or children; this is a deceptively easy escape. Eventually we will have to face our own needs or we will feel empty. As with men, our individual identities should be acknowledged. Identifying ourselves through our children's success is not enough. It is reductive.

Also implicit in the "grannymom" nickname was a negative approach to aging. People were making fun of me for being old, yet doing something that younger women did. In some ways, I feel like ageism is the last frontier in America; it is still somewhat acceptable to discriminate against people, or at least make fun of them, for being "over the hill."

AGEISM: THE LAST FRONTIER

Despite the numerous 'waves' of feminism that have broken down barriers to equality, society still has a long way to go to catch up with women. Today we are longer-lived and, due to an array of different factors, feel younger, more vital, and more energetic than ever—particularly during what have traditionally been our 'twilight years'. Given the judgments about older women, which manifest themselves in both brazen and more subtle ways, it's unsurprising that so many women lie about their age.

In all the negative comments about my age that accompanied my high-profile multiple birth, I started to sense a subtext of *fear*. Age may be the last taboo, the last quality it's become acceptable to pass judgement on, especially when looks and fertility are involved. Here I was having IVF at sixty, and women asked condescendingly whether it was because I wanted to seem younger than I was, or whether I was courting attention in order to showcase my glamorousness. Some even accused me of doing all this in a ploy to get my own reality TV, or as a grasping attempt to get a movie made about my life. Implicit in this critique was the idea that I should be ashamed to be proudly in public as a sixty-year-old doing something that younger women typically do. I was overstepping my bounds, in a sense, and for some reason that evoked great unease.

Women were afraid of my confidence, my willingness to embark on an undeniably tiring eighteen-year project, because they felt I should be put in my place; perhaps I was older than they were and, looking nervously toward the future, they were afraid of being judged like I was, and so expressed their fear as biting angriness.

Many television-viewers, article-readers, and commenters on Web sites called my twins' birth "superficial." It was far from that. In fact, I'd spend decades studying the impact of career, relationships, and family life on women's happiness. My decision to have the twins at sixty had been deeply considered, taking into account my desires as well as those of my close family. I may have blonde hair and wear high boots over skinny jeans, but this decision wasn't about vanity.

Whether it was my intent to do so or not, thanks to the media attention the birth of these two wonderful boys has made a statement. Its effects will be long-lived. Now, *even older* at sixty-nine, I want to share with you some thoughts and perspectives. In addition to relating my personal story, I will describe what I think are the wider implications of my multiple birth at sixty; after all, having practiced psychotherapy for several decades after getting my PhD in Psychology, I've seen a lot and analyzed it scrupulously. Whether or not you choose to follow my example and have an untraditionally late-in-life birth, I hope that some of my thoughts will give you some insight — and some *company* in navigating the complicated, exciting issues that surround the issue of age.

One thing is for sure: in getting older, there is nothing to be afraid of. It may sound obvious, but so many women–when asked how old they are–subtly "twist the truth" or demure or flat-out refuse to answer. And so many of us are guilty of trying to bring down others by saying things like, "Ugh, she's trying to appear younger. Who does she think she is?"

Being over sixty–or over seventy, or thirty or forty–is nothing to be ashamed of. Rather, it is something to be excited about. I decided to become a new mother at sixty, and many people were shocked and outraged. But I also decided to reinvent myself as a media pundit, a public speaker, and a participant in my community. I ran around with my twins, but I also began a new life of my own–one I was determined to live on my own terms. People seemed transfixed by my age, and so I began to explore this issue through the lens of my work as a psychotherapist. And I began to speak about what I had learned, louder and prouder and more strongly than ever before.

2

Pressure and Ambition

WOMEN WHO MAKE CHANGES CHANGE HISTORY. I'm not just talking about having babies at sixty. I'm talking about achieving our dreams, filling our lives with love, and reinventing ourselves . . . at any age we please.

All these dreams-come-true, great loves, and big achievements are ours for the taking, it's true. But life is complicated, and we don't exist in a vacuum. Our parents, friends, partners, bosses, and our children are all complicated beings with their own desires. Sometimes they want things from us that we can't readily give them—not without compromising something we hold dear.

During my childhood and early adulthood, when I got married and became a new mother in my late twenties, and well afterward as I tried to pursue career goals while acting as the "perfect" wife and mother . . . compromising my own dreams in order to take care of others was a constant theme. I felt pressure all the time, and from all directions.

I sensed that I was giving up a piece of myself, sometimes vaguely and other times more acutely, throughout my life. Other people have always needed things from me, and I gave them what they needed right away, often without considering the impact it would have on me. I didn't know how to put myself first.

Often I felt very alone. But later in life, I came to the ever-so-comforting understanding that almost everyone feels that way sometimes. And as women, we feel that way a whole lot of the time.

SHOULD I BE SMILING, TOO?

One afternoon when I was in my early thirties, I found myself standing in line at the supermarket behind a young woman, my age or even a little younger. She looked incredibly happy. Her eyes were bright and her smile natural as she placed groceries on the conveyor belt—helped by her three young children. I had two kids of my own, Jaeson and Alana (who were equally helpful). But I knew my smile was labored, and that somehow, despite my love for my son and daughter, I was feeling crushingly bored.

Why was this other woman so happy while I felt discontented? Was she *really* happy? Was I happy, but somehow numb to my own contentment?

A sinking feeling suddenly overtook my body. I had a big, rambling house and a family, and could afford anything I wanted from the supermarket's shelves. Despite having what I thought I wanted—at least, what my very traditional mother had always intimated that I *should* want—I felt, in that moment, empty and somehow bankrupt.

Was this "it"? What was I missing?

Standing on that line, I thought back to a morning a couple of days earlier when, as I was getting off the elevator in my apartment building, I bumped into a neighbor. "Where are you going?" she had asked me.

"I'm going to school," I said proudly. I was pursuing graduate school in psychology.

"Well, *I* would never leave my small children with a sitter," she sneered. This cut through me like a knife, and as I made my way to school I felt somehow ashamed. Did she think I was a bad mother? *Was* I a bad mother?

Then, it hit me: that unsettling feeling I was experiencing at that supermarket came from a fear of letting people down.

The generation in which I grew up, and my parents in particular, told me to stay home: my big achievement in life, according to them, would be to marry well and have children. The mother radiating ebullient joy at the checkout, the neighbor who would *never* leave her small children in another's care, and *my own mother* all seemed to tell me that motherhood should be enough. Why, then, did I feel the need to pursue graduate school? And why was there still this empty hole inside of me that was growing difficult to ignore?

I went home, unpacked the groceries, and thought some more. Two choices presented themselves. I could bury this almost-shocking feeling of discontent, the dismal questioning of whether this was all there was. I'd bury it, and go on with my life, be an attentive wife and mother, keeping my family well-fed, clean, and cheerful. I would never mention it again.

The other option was to take the feeling seriously. Rather than keeping it inside, I would confide in others who might feel this way. After all, I had studied psychology for many years. I had the tools to analyze this feeling, and a network of people I'd met in graduate school who could help me unpack the questions.

The choice was a no-brainer: into research mode I went.

REACHING OUT AND RESEARCHING

Foiling my sense of isolation, I reached out and searched for subjects by sending seven hundred postcards throughout New York City's boroughs and the surrounding suburbs. I believed my "Is this all there is?" feeling related to the fact that I was supposed to be overcome with wedded bliss, and had two children; this was what I thought I had always wanted, but something felt 'off.' I wanted to collect a large sample group of women who were in relationships. And eventually I had one, three hundred women strong.

I hired a statistician through my graduate school and set about compiling in-depth surveys focusing on life satisfaction in relation to career and marriage. We asked for some basic information on family background (parents' occupations, and their status as still-married or divorced). We asked for their educational history, and included numerous questions about their work: Had they been employed before? Were they working now?

We took it a step further with questions like, "If you are divorced, do you feel that your entering the work force was a factor which led to the divorce?" The majority of the survey focused on the marriage relationship. Women rated twenty-five statements about their sex lives on a scale of one to five, and evaluated the frequency of whether, for instance, "the two of you ever sit down just to talk things over." Survey by survey, a broad spectrum of women's levels of satisfaction with their relationships would emerge. I hoped that the results would shine a light on why I felt like something was missing.

While I waited for the surveys to be completed, I thought some more about why something felt missing in my life–a life that to passersby looked picture-perfect. Hidden among the hustle of the day-to-day, I often harbored a sense of malaise, which sometimes felt like boredom or dullness. I kept asking myself, *Is this it?* I thought about my son and my daughter–adorable, beautiful, vibrant. I thought about my house, decorated to my tastes. I thought about my husband, beside whom I'd been for so long it felt like second nature.

Once when we were in upstate New York, he asked, "Why are you hiking on these pebbles when you can walk on this smooth road?" I didn't know how to answer him, but somehow walking on that path made sense to me.

Things could have been smooth and easy for me, but I wanted something different. I did not always know how to answer people, or precisely how to define what I wanted. When I was a young mother who should have been jubilant, but was asking herself, "Is this all there is?" pretty much every day, I thought of all these things. And most of all I thought about my past.

"NO. NO, NO"

Growing up in Cleveland, Ohio, I was eager to please my parents. Hardworking, I decided I wanted to be a camp counselor at twelve and—lacking a camp nearby—embarked on the ambitious project of setting up my own camp for local children. In school I studied hard, participated in activities, was polite around adults, and did everything I thought was expected of me.

Yet for some reason, I was always told I *could not*. "No. No, no" echoed in my ears. As a teenager, "No, you can't go to New York to become a salesgirl," my mother told me—even after I was praised by my employer for selling an insane number of encyclopedias in my teens.

This was not my only "endeavor." At fourteen, I had sold real estate on the phone. At sixteen, I'd worked at a clothing store before moving on to those encyclopedias. Nineteen was my year of ballroom dancing; I took lots of classes at the local Fred Astaire studio, became an instructor, and was invited to tour with the school on the high seas.

"No, you can't go on a cruise," was my mother's response.

I wanted to be on television, so begged my parents to let me pursue a career in acting. When I asked my mother why I was not allowed to pursue the spotlight, or why she vetoed the exciting things I was invited to do, her remark cut through me like a knife: "I was never able to do these things, so why should you?"

I made some bad decisions all by myself, too. One day a man on the street stopped me. He was flanked by two others; all were handsome and grinning at me. "Do you want to work for me?" My heart fluttered, as even at that age I recognized a stroke of luck when I saw it. But this time *I* said "no." I knew my parents wouldn't allow it. When I came home that night, I realized how right I was: my mother had sent the police to look for me as I had not called at the usual time.

Later I saw that handsome man on TV: he was Mike Douglas, a famous host in Cleveland. Grudgingly accepting that I had given up a job of a lifetime, I started working with medical devices down the street from my house as I attended college during the evening a commuter student.

MOVING TO THE CITY

Finally, after graduating, my parents gave their seal of approval to my desire to go out into the world and explore. I was at last allowed to move to Manhattan, but only if I lived with a roommate of their choosing. She happened to be extremely religious. We did not get along, but I dared not tell my mother, fearing that she would order me to return home. And so I tried to stay out of the apartment as much as I could.

Determined to support myself, I got a job at Bellevue Hospital and worked in the operating room cleaning instruments. I was so nervous every day that I broke out in hives. But earning a living there was preferable to getting my parents' checks in the mail. They moved me up to the blood gas department where I measured blood for oxygen. There, I found out about the Respiratory Department, applied, and began to work there instead.

Living in Manhattan felt so right. I did not want to go home. And I believed that in order to keep avoiding my parents' demands that I return home, I would have to meet a man.

One weekend, I attended a singles event in Grossinger's, an upstate resort for Jewish singles. (It was like a 1968 precursor to today's JDate.) I remember buying a ticket to a Short Line bus; at the ticket window I paid the salesperson in coins in order to get to the Catskills. Dumbfounded — used to the very rich, who would peel off big bills left and right — he said, "Go home. You will never make it there."

That gnawed away at my confidence, but I wanted badly to meet someone and so I continued on the journey. I checked in and met my roommate, who had a spinal deformity and was so unconfident that she didn't want to talk to me or leave the room. I prepared to spend the weekend on my own.

At lunch one day, I was sitting alone at a big table when a young man walked up and asked if I would like to join him.

How romantic, I thought. The dining room was full, and I could see that at least one woman was not-so-subtly interested in him. But he gave up the chance to lunch with anyone else.

Not only did that go well, but he and I wound up riding back to New York together on the bus. When he removed his scarf from around his neck to give it to me, I melted, and I knew his kindness is what sold me. We were engaged three months later, and three months after that, Ken and I were married. I was twenty-two.

Even though I barely had the money for a bus ticket, I definitely got what I had gone to Grossinger's to pursue. I had always been told that who I was going to marry, not my own accomplishments, would be the big thing in my life. And so I walked down the aisle in a dress that made me look like a Barbie doll, and I felt accomplished. Only when I look back at the photos do I recognize a look of concern on my face. It wasn't that I felt I was marrying the wrong person; instead, I think the look on my face reflects the fear that I was rushing into something before I had the chance to really find myself, to be selfish and pursue my own dreams. That day, lots of thoughts were swirling through my head. Sorting them out was the hard part.

My new husband began a demanding law school program, and I continued to work odd jobs to pay his tuition, textbooks, and living expenses as well as my own. For the most part, I worked long hours as the assistant to an orthodontist. I always took care to put the money on a table, so he would not feel demeaned by my handing him money. In the same vein, I loved seeing my mother happy when I'd buy her things like clothing or face cream; I'd anticipate her happiness over what I had bought her, and that made me very happy. My mother was happy with me, as I settled into domestic life.

Although life was busy, I felt pressure to become a mother; in fact, I imagined a stigma against wives without babies. Soon I was pregnant.

I gave birth to Jaeson, a beautiful and gifted son. He excelled in everything he did, but being a young mother, I was not aware that it could have been any different. Four years later, I gave birth to a beautiful and talented daughter, Alana, who has always wanted what was best for me.

But as the years rolled by I felt another sort of pressure. My husband started to suggest that I was, to put it bluntly, "just a housewife." It was like he was putting me down, and I didn't like that one bit. Still, I internalized his words.

PURSUING A DREAM

I had always been interested in people, wondering what lay beneath the surface of their expressions and why they acted the way they did. I decided to pursue one of my dreams: to become a psychologist. I enrolled in classes at a psychoanalytic institute in New York, and then finished my bachelor's of science before starting a PhD.

But there wasn't any joy for me from my elders, especially my mother-in-law. "You're just getting your PhD because it is fun," she would say. Here was a woman who had never worked a day in her life outside the home. She even had a full-time housekeeper and cook when her children were no longer home. *Oh, right, it's fun to study statistics and research while my children are sleeping and I'm near exhaustion. Great fun*, I thought. But I just smiled and hid my hurt deep inside, staying quiet.

I later found in my research that women who did not feel a sense of accomplishment felt threatened by other women who succeeded. It clashed badly with my upbringing: I was brought up to take care of others, and the women in my husband's family were brought up to be taken care of. It was a perfect fit. Or maybe it was a terrible fit.

Going to school full-time while trying to be the perfect wife and mother was hard juggling work, and even though I was not entirely supported in doing it, my intuition told me that I needed to be doing something for myself, something that took me outside the home every day and which had nothing to do with my husband or young children.

At four o'clock one morning, while I typed away on my dissertation with bleary eyes, my computer crashed. The screen went blank, and with the heaviest heart I had ever experienced it dawned on me that I had not saved my work. That morning, I lost my term paper. And I gave up on the degree program.

I finished my PhD through a program that would let me do the coursework from home; I ran around with my son and daughter between tests and papers. When I was done and started using the "Dr." in front of my name, my husband would scoff, "That's just a PhD—it means nothing."

From our home, I set up a private practice and started building a client base. When my husband wanted to move to a different area, I stood up for my professional self and argued that we should stay put. We did stay in that house, and I continued to see patients as Jaeson and Alana grew.

My husband knew how to push my buttons. "You just want to be a housewife," he would still insist from time to time, a hint of teasing in his voice. To me, it was far from funny. There was a need to break every mold and boundary I could perceive, to keep growing, changing, learning, and trying new things.

3

Surviving, and What My Mother Didn't Say

My PARENTS HAD REAL CHALLENGES. THEIR EARLY lives were violent and characterized by the need for physical survival, to the point where I'm guessing they did not have a lot of time to think about whether they were fulfilling their true potentials, finding their voices, and evolving and changing—all things that I had worried about when I came of age. That look on my face—of questioning, of concern for my expression of individuality—which I now see in old photographs, as I walked down the aisle in that dream-come-true wedding dress? When my parents got married, they had other things on their minds.

Now, as I think about what was going through my head when I became a mother in my late twenties, and as I contemplate what it meant to do it again in my fifties and (shockingly!) yet again in my sixties, it is interesting to recognize that times are changing. My parents and I slid into adulthood and domestic life under very different circumstances. As our society progresses, we have more options and more freedom to choose how our lives will unfold.

My parents suffered for their religion, and for their determination make the best life for their family. They overcame real obstacles, which my children can only dream of (and I am thankful for that).

When I was in my twenties, I went out with my friends to see a movie in which the main characters were so deprived that they ate worms in their soup. Many families were squeezed together into one room. The temperature was forty-five degrees below zero. I walked out of that movie before it ended. I could not bear the suffering.

I told my father about the movie. "Frieda, I lived that life," he told me. I had had no idea; my father had always seemed so calm and collected.

I asked him to tell me more, and started to tape-record it. I wrote some of it down. That tape contains some crying; he often spoke through his tears, in Yiddish, the language he knew best. Even when he cried, he kept talking—though I often had to stop the tape and take a break. I found it hard to even *hear* about the kind of challenges my parents lived through. They were, in many ways, extremely tough people who faced an entirely different set of challenges than I did.

SAYING GOODBYE

My parents were brought up in the same small Polish town. Children played in the streets. Among their Jewish community, even the poorest people dressed up to go to temple every Shabbat. There, they prayed and celebrated together.

"Bang, bang" was my father's rendition of the bombs that he remembers blasting through the air and reverberating through his neighborhood one dark night. With *his* father, he ran into the synagogue and rescued the Torah scrolls. When they came out there were bodies all around them. The war was escalating.

By morning, most of the houses in town were just bare shells. By this point, my father and mother were planning to get married. My mother's family had the opportunity to escape Poland for Russia, which they thought would be safer. And so my father's father made the quick decision that he would send him away with his sweetheart's family. In the morning he told my father matter-of-factly, "It is with a heavy heart that I must tell you goodbye."

My grandfather knew that if the young people were married, his son could go with them to Russia and that he would be more likely to survive. In order to protect his son, he had to send him away from a home that wartime was making more and more dangerous. I cannot imagine having to make such a heart-rending choice.

My grandfather found a student at the local yeshiva on the street, the first person he saw with the ability to marry people. He ordered the student to marry my parents. My father could see the tears in my grandfather's eyes as he bid them farewell and sent them away. My father did not have the chance to say goodbye to his own mother.

Several months later, my father—newly married and living in Russia, protected for the time being from the bombings—could endure the estrangement from his birth family no longer. He had to go back and find his parents. His bride's father wished him well and handed him one hundred *slotus*. He jumped on a train, hiding behind a post when the German soldier asked for tickets as he did not know when he would need the tiny sum for something else. Then he jumped off, ran up a fence, ripped his pants and found a man with a wagon that seemed to be filled with hay, but in fact concealed a false bottom where he could hide, traveling across the Russian border and into the Polish town unseen.

"Click, click, click" is the sound my father remembers hearing then. It was the sound of bayonets striking through the hay. He lay completely still, knowing that the slightest movement—even a deep breath—could get him killed. When he finally heard the commander yell "go" and was confident the men had retreated, he made his escape. The first person he happened upon was a young boy, to whom he paid fifty *slotus* to help him cross the border, which involved walking across a river.

Before they got there, the boy ran away and left my father on his own. There along the border he saw a lady and her two children. She begged him to carry her over the river. She was obese, but my father, who was only five feet tall, helped her across before going back for the children.

When he stumbled back to his village, he found his mother gravely ill with typhoid fever and his father missing. He went to the commander and asked for help, as his mother was dying.

"We don't treat Jews," the commander responded. My father got so angry that he swiped his hand across the commander's desk and spilled his inkwell. The brazen gesture was a fatal move: he was thrown in jail, his mother died quickly, and his father was soon killed for refusing to shave his beard, a sign of religious devotion. My father went back to Russia a broken man, now knowing the fates of his parents.

DEATH AND NEW LIFE IN SIBERIA

Months later, when he least expected it, he heard another click of a gun at his forehead. One more click and he would surely be dead. He looked up at a young soldier staring down at him. Instead of killing him, the soldier took my father, my mother, and my mother's parents to a waiting station, where they would be transported to a labor camp in Siberia.

Several days later, a train came and took them through a maze of small towns they did not recognize. In one town he saw people carrying armfuls of bread. Luckily the train stopped. My father snuck out and ran to the merchant, shouting, "I want an armful of bread!" The man asked whether my father had any money, and he responded that he didn't. Everyone laughed. "I'll pay for him," a woman in line said. So my father went back to the train with an armful of bread. That night everyone celebrated.

The next stop was Siberia, where the temperature often dipped to forty-five degrees below zero. The snowfall measured all the way to my father's hips and he was put to work taking out tree stumps. My parents were allotted slices of bread each, every day. One day, my father says, my mother wanted to surprised him so she brought him his slice. But on the way, she nibbled at it. "I ate the whole slice," she reported sadly. "Better you than me," my father replied.

By his own account, he was quite the hero when it came to bread. But his feats didn't end there.

At one point, he says, he was given a pair of boots that were too small. When he spoke up, he was thrown in jail. Then he was charged with guarding a ship, which necessitated jumping from one cliff to another—until one day he fell. "He's dead, he's dead!" everyone yelled. Then a woman saw him breathing, and he was sent to the hospital. There he ate real meals for the first time in months. On his way back from the hospital he was pulled back to camp behind a horse in three feet of snow, for three whole days, in what he described to me as "excruciating pain." It smacked of the "uphill both ways" tall tales that children are often told—except this time, in a work camp in Siberia, it was probably true.

My father had an escape plan. He and several other men put the women and children in a wagon and in the middle of the night they snuck out. The next afternoon a helicopter hovered over them. It landed and three commanders came out and fenced them in.

"Who wants to tell us what happened? We need eight people," the commanders said. Eight people timidly raised their hands. They were sent out to the back. "Bang, bang, bang, bang, bang, bang, bang, bang," my father recited. Many of his memories of youth involved weapons being cocked at him, ready to fire. Everyone else in the wagon, my parents among them, were sent back to the freezing cold camp.

Death was all around my parents, but life also began. My mother soon became pregnant. She gave birth to a son, who died of starvation soon after he came into the world. And then the same thing happened to a second son. Next, she had a girl—my sister, Goldie—who lived; according to my father, they had found a rare, raw potato to feed her shortly after birth, which made a difference.

When Goldie was three years old, my father was ordered to serve in the Polish army. While he was standing in line to join the service, Goldie called him over to say goodbye. Knowing it could be the last time he ever saw her, my father thought back to his father's farewell in Poland, which had always haunted him. He decided to risk the commanders' wrath and step out of line. They embraced, he reluctantly rejoined the line at the end ... and when his turn came, my father experienced yet twist of fate when the commander put his hand in front of him and yelled, "We are finished!" They needed no more soldiers. For what seemed like the umpteenth time, my father's life was saved, this time by his daughter.

In 1944, World War II was finally declared to be over. American soldiers came and took the Nazis away in trucks. After having been in the camp for seven years, my parents were sent to Russia, where my sister Rachel was born. Soon after they were sent to Germany, where I was born.

Shortly after I was born, the hospital made a grave mistake. They switched me with another infant, a boy. My mother noticed right away, but it took her three days to say anything. At first, she thought I might be better off with the other woman, who seemed to have more money than she had. But then she decided to keep me instead.

Four children in tow (a younger brother's birth followed mine), my parents departed for a new world.

"America or Australia?" the man from the Jewish Immigration said.

"America," my father said proudly.

"New York, or . . .?"

"Cleveland," was my dad's answer.

The Jewish Federation helped our family to get settled in Ohio. Quickly my father found work as a tailor. When he brought home his first American paycheck, my mother celebrated with food for Shabbat.

Ask your mother or grandmother where she spent most of her life, and many will give the same answer: cleaning, cooking, washing dishes, and taking care of children. And as I child I had a rich life, a life full of caring, support, and passion. For that I have always been grateful. We celebrated holidays and everyday events together. There was always happiness in our house

My mother was the same. For hours and hours and hours every day and night, she prepared gefilte fish from chopping up carp and white fish; filled another entire fish with stuffing; and cooked chicken soup, homemade noodles, stuffed chicken, stuffed derma (the intestines of a cow, my favorite), potato kugel, and compote for dessert. Sometime she made a salad to keep things on the healthy side, but of course we drenched it with salad dressing. It was a far cry from the worms that had occasionally been found in my parents' soup in Siberia.

I remember her mentioning one evening that the lady across the street had an unusual habit: she would sit and eat with her family at dinner. My family was shocked.

"Who serves them?" we asked.

My mother took me shopping with her. She bought eggs in a store that only sold eggs. "Give me the cracked eggs," she would say proudly—and then to me: "Because you see Frieda a penny with a penny makes a dollar." She even plucked the feathers off the chicken she bought, so she could save money. When she went to the butcher's shop, she would insist on going into the freezer and picking the meat before he chopped it for hamburgers. She would not buy chopped meat. I even remember tagging along with her to buy two large fish that were swimming around in someone's bathtub; we carried them home in a plastic bag.

My parents were the first of their friends to become American citizens. They were also the first to buy a house; I guess my mother was right about those cracked eggs.

My father told me his story of heroism, wrenching goodbyes, and near-death experiences in war-torn Europe. My mother's big feats, it seemed, were accomplished inside the four walls of our house. With four children— Goldie, Rachel, and I were joined by a younger brother—

she seemed to spend every waking hour cooking and cleaning.

My story is not unique. When we ask our parents or our grandparents to describe their lives, often they will talk about dodging danger and serving others. While my father remembers his own heroism, my mother preferred to stay quiet about her feelings about the past and instead focused on the people around her. She was focused on meeting everyone else's needs.

WHAT SHE DIDN'T SAY

My mother talked a lot about how important it was to be a good wife and mother. But I now suspect that she also sent me unconscious messages which told me a story about her private frustrations. I certainly picked up on some resentments, possibly about ambitions unfulfilled. But then again, my parents' generation had so-called *real* problems, issues of life and death. Anything else was a luxury.

Among the clients I have seen as a psychotherapist, I often noticed how children would pick up on their parents' unconscious messages. Sometimes these messages would produce a feeling of conflictedness.

Today, as mothers, we are able to do something that many of our own mothers couldn't: we can best serve not just ourselves, but also our families by making sure we do not bottle things up inside. We can make sure we fulfill our own ambitions and explore our own desires in addition to being mothers. Having children later in life is a good way to do that.

Defying the odds, my parents had dodged being killed in the Holocaust, which claimed the lives of six million Jews, and three million more because they were homosexuals, gypsies, elderly, or disabled.

Talk to members of previous generations and you'll see: many of them have stories of surviving against all odds. From the bombing of their village to worms in their soup, they endured and fought for everything they had. When I finally heard my father's story, I thought: *if they could survive all this, then surely I should be able to survive absolutely anything.*

But then again, today we want more than just to survive. A thriving family, a strong marriage *and* self-actualization: I confess that I want it all. Am I greedy? I don't think so, merely practical.

My mother's needs were repressed and other's needs were exaggerated. This common thread ran through the lives of many women in my family. On the other hand, from my perspective, it seems that the women on my husband's side of the family became dependent on others, expressing their own needs openly but depending on others, rather than themselves, to fulfill them.

Today, many women struggle with the challenge of making their needs known while also catering to those of others; I see it all the time in my practice. There are many women out there who, after reaching their mid-thirties or so, find themselves somewhere they would rather not be. And very often, this struggle is linked to motherhood.

In my practice, I often see that when my female clients are no longer immersed in child care, and when they assess their lives, they find themselves in less-than-desirable relationships, with no goals of their own and in need of self-fulfillment. "What happened to me along the way?" they ask. These women want to realize their dreams. And from what I have seen among the clients and among my own friends and acquaintances in the suburbs, these women often divorce, breaking away from controlling and abusive husbands, attempting to find a way to fulfill themselves.

But we no longer live in my parents' world. Thankfully, more and more women are holding prestigious positions in all levels from politics to business to professional careers. The assertiveness that is required in the workplace is transferring itself into the home. These women are being treated differently at home. Their husbands can no longer ignore their needs because they are capable of getting their needs met on their own. Reproductive technology that allows us to have children later in life goes hand in hand with this progress.

When a child sees his or her mother as a strong and independent person, that child learns how to have a family, relationship and career. But most of all, by seeing their mother happy, they are free to make themselves happy. I hope that I have projected this kind of thing to my older children *and* my younger ones grow up with a mother who feels secure in who she is and free to express herself, rather than frustrated or bottled up.

4

Pregnancy at Fifty-Three

IN MY FORTIES, I WAS A MOTHER OF A SON AND DAUGHTER who were rapidly growing up. But I longed for something more. And for me, that something more involved becoming a mother again. How to explain it?

My desire to have another child ran so deep that while on vacation I found myself wondering about a pregnant young woman who was working as a hostess in the hotel dining room. *I wonder if she really wants that baby,* I thought. *Should I ask her?* At that point, I figured I was going off the deep end. I told my husband and kids about it, and they, too, thought I was crazy. Of course, I didn't really want to seize this young woman's baby; I just wanted one for myself.

The feeling was so strong that when I saw the word "adopt" on an "Adopt a Highway" sign, I got excited. Interestingly, I did not remember having experienced such a strong urge to be a mother when I was younger. Maybe being older and more contented, having my own mind, was a better time to have children than when I was younger and needed to find myself in life, and on some level my body knew that.

My husband and I decided to try for another child. I began a course of IVF and soon I found out I was pregnant. Three months into the pregnancy, I experienced extreme physical pain. I drove my husband to the airport that day, and he insisted I walk with him through the terminal. He did not support my desire to stay home due to the pain. I cried when I saw the plane take off.

"Don't worry. He'll be back soon," said a flight attendant. "Have you recently gotten married?"

She didn't know that I was not crying for him but for myself—and the fear of losing my child three months into my pregnancy. Somehow, I felt that it would happen, and I was right. I miscarried that night.

EARLY OPTIONS FOR LATE MOTHERHOOD

Two years later, I was told that while my chance of getting pregnant was only fifteen percent, my hormone level was good enough that my chances could be much greater. But my husband was worried about the fertility shots and whether they might be carcinogenic.

I found myself thinking more and more about other options, especially adoption and using a surrogate. Childbirth when I was younger had been a tortuous affair; I didn't want to go through it again.

But I found myself faced with a dilemma. A professional colleague of mine had adopted and was having constant problems with her child. Then when my adoption case worker told me about her personal pain caused by her own adopted son, I knew that I needed some kind of guarantee that my own outcome would be better.

I also called a woman who had adopted two children from Russia. She was in her late forties. When I told her about my desire to adopt, she scoffed, "Why do you want to adopt if you already have two grown children?" Not only was she not helpful, but she laughed at my request.

I reached out to a clinic in Pennsylvania that would work with me to hire a surrogate. I got a call from a young mother who had four children. My husband had a bad feeling about this young woman's intentions. Around Christmastime that year, she reached out to me and said she needed money for her children; without telling anyone, even my husband, sent her one hundred dollars. I never called her again, not because I thought it wouldn't work, but because my husband felt uncomfortable with it and I suspected he might be right because of her secretiveness and request for money.

Next, we went to an agency in Manhattan. There, we were shown pictures and read histories of women interested in becoming surrogates for $45,000. We would have baby. I felt I was on a roll. We made plans to go out to dinner to celebrate our anniversary with the children. But that day, my husband delivered some news that I found sobering. As an attorney, he felt that this agency could put us in jeopardy because it did not meet the proper legal standards. My heart sank. Was he trying to sabotage our family plans on purpose?

We then sought out "Richard," a man who talked to us for three hours on the phone, until three in the morning. He would be able to get us the child we wanted—but for a fee of $100,000. He could give us the names of judges, doctors, actors, millionaires who would confirm to us how pleased they were to have worked with him. Not only that, he brought babies to people of all ages—even a man who was seventy-two and his wife who was in her fifties. We called the numbers he gave us, and we spoke to interesting and happy people. But at the end of the process we decided that we shouldn't have to spend all that money to have a baby through a rather murky process.

And then we took part in a meeting for prospective adopted parents. Some had already adopted. One was a teacher, a single woman who looked to be way beyond her baby-bearing years. Another woman, someone in her forties, had just adopted a baby and insisted that we would have no regrets. The guest speaker showed us a picture of her twenty-something son and told us that she and her husband loved him no less than their birth daughter. I was very moved. But again, my husband had second thoughts. And so we said "no."

I tried for a while to put the strong desire to give birth again out of my mind, and to go on with my life. But the desire remained.

One day, a few months after seeing those guest speakers, I read an article about a cutting-edge fertility procedure for older women, where a woman's egg is mixed with the male's sperm in a Petri dish. My husband could not get out of this one. And we wouldn't have to pay any money up front, only when they were ready to implant the embryo—and by then he would have no choice. It was the only way. I had made up my mind that through this process, I would have another child.

Donor eggs? Choosing the right partner in your life is very important for a lot of reasons, but a big one is that it will go a long way in determining what kind of children you will have. Picking a donor egg or donor sperm is similar in that you are picking the right person to help produce a child.

So first, we met the doctor; insurance covered that. Then I had to take some medication that wasn't too expensive, and insurance covered some of that. The next step was an in vitro procedure, and that required money up front. By that time, I had already put my body through so much preparation for pregnancy that it was hard for my husband to back off. In total, it cost us around twenty thousand dollars

It worked. At fifty-three years old, I became pregnant with a boy—and my husband could not have been happier with "his" decision.

HOW PREGNANCY WAS DIFFERENT THIS TIME

To avoid complications in my pregnancy, I was treated in a preventative way. I went to someone who specialized in complicated pregnancies. I had my heart monitored, I had the baby's heart monitored, and I was given special blood tests to check abnormalities. Luckily, none came to the surface.

On a personal level, I was treated differently by my doctors: this time, they spoke to me as an equal. It may have been my age, but most likely times had changed since I had a baby twenty-seven years before. For instance, they would explain the medical side of things to me, whereas in the past they expected such terminology to go right over my head and kept me largely in the dark.

And emotionally, this time around, I felt more relaxed. I may have harbored fears about the baby's health and discomfort while pregnant at fifty-three, but they do not stand out in my memory. Such anxious feelings were much more vivid when I was pregnant in my late twenties.

I found a sense of levity, in fact. Seeing the baby through ultrasound was my biggest source of entertainment. The young nurses heard how old I was and said they "couldn't believe" that I looked so healthy, so in shape, and so well groomed. I guess they expected me to look worse than everyone else.

But best of all, I was able to share my experiences with my husband. Everyone seemed to expect him to be more involved than he was last time around, and he was happy to take on this role, going into the doctors' offices with me. He did not act like pregnancy was just "my thing."

We weren't alone. When we'd go to the doctor, I'd notice that about half the people in the waiting room were women and half their husbands. Phrases like "We are having a baby" caught my attention. Having a child had become more of a team effort. Men were taking responsibility for their wives' pregnancies, and that I liked.

As I got larger, my female clients started to notice. Some of them were moved to consider motherhood at a later age, too. One of my patients unsuccessfully tried in vitro fertilization at age forty-six. I had helped to improve the health of some of my patients' relationships, and therefore I saw many beautiful children come out of these reunions. But this was different. These women didn't realize that they still had the opportunity to have another child or two, and they were fascinated with my pregnancy, since I was often older than they were.

There came a time when I no longer could lift milk containers at the supermarket—so I had to ask the clerk to lift them for me. At first, I said it was my back. Then, when I could no longer hide my pregnancy, I tearfully broke down and told her I was pregnant. She handled my request in an understanding and compassionate manner, and I was grateful that she was not shocked by me. I was pleasantly surprised at her matter-of-fact reaction.

During the last stages of pregnancy, when I thought it would be too uncomfortable going out of the house and being seen, I instead felt empowered and became indifferent to the message I was giving with my body. One day, I was in the supermarket picking corn and saw a young lady who was also choosing corn and who also was pregnant. She glanced at me, then stared at me. To this day I don't know if she felt we had something in common or that it was strange that we had *that* something in common.

MOTHERHOOD AGAIN, AT FIFTY-THREE

When I gave birth to my son Ari at fifty-three, there was no publicity blitz—but I was still keenly aware that I was older than the average mother. In fact, there were times when I felt downright self-conscious, even embarrassed, about being older than the young moms I anticipated seeing during school-runs.

Something unexpected happened, however. In my everyday life, no one seemed to know, or cared all that much, that I was older than the average new mother. In fact, a surprisingly high number of Ari's school-mates' mothers were around my age. In order to fit into what they thought was the mold of motherhood—or just because they wanted to be seen as younger, associating some kind of virtue with it—some had lied about it.

While most around me were accepting, my adult children were far less happy. Alana said: "I will never talk to you again, and I am definitely moving out of the house. You are too old." And Jaeson said: "If you want more children why don't you wait, and you will have grandchildren?"

TOO OLD?

"Aren't you too old to become a new mother?"

I was asked this question over and over, and thought about it long and hard.

I didn't think so, and neither did lots of other women. Although I got a lot of criticism, women in my life also expressed friendly curiosity. And once my case was publicized, I got a lot of letters from women around the world who identified with my later-than-usual pregnancy.

Often they wanted to know how I became pregnant, and were interested in doing the same.

At thirty-five, I had become pregnant and miscarried. Even back then, people had something to say about my age; I was told that I had miscarried due to being "old." At fifty-three, I knew that I really wanted that baby but was conflicted about what society told me. I was too old. When I was forty-five, I asked a doctor if I was too old.

"But will I not fit in?" I said. Secretly I was worried that I *looked* too old to be a new mother.

"*That's* not the problem," he responded. "Do you feel you can handle a baby? Staying up late? Taking care of him all day?"

But that was not my concern. In my mind, it was already a given. I knew that I would delight in caring for a child. After all, when any of my patients brought in their children, my energy level went up. I knew that the extra work was nothing compared to the joy I felt in seeing these children.

Still, I kept my mission a secret from my patients. I thought they would be turned off to my plight. After all, many of them were my age, talking about retirement or moving to a warmer climate. But as pregnancy changed my body, I continued to fit in the same clothing. To my surprise, my pregnancy was not visible to others until the last three months.

My patients trusted my judgment. "If you feel you want another child, then you must know what you are doing," was a sentiment several expressed said, adding that they couldn't do it, that it was too much work or that they wouldn't want to do it. Said one: "This is *my* time. I deserve it. After all, I already put in all the work necessary to bring up a family, so why on earth would I want to do it again?" No one said, to my face anyway, that they thought I would be sorry or that I was doing the wrong thing.

I almost forgot the mailman. He saw the balloons outside on the mailbox, balloons that I displayed for my son Ari's bris. "Congratulations," he said. "Did your daughter have a baby?" "No," I said, "it was me." "You mean it was your daughter." "No, it was me." "Are you sure? For a second, I thought you said it was you?" "Yes." He held onto the door as if he were going to fall over. "Did you do it on purpose?" he asked breathlessly. "Well, congratulations," he said, clearly bewildered.

A year later, when he saw me walking outside with my son, he said it was the best thing I ever did. I heard the same thing from shopkeepers, clerks, my manicurist, the people at my temple. They had grandmothers who had their babies late in life, and they wished that they had had a baby later in life. But now it was a done deal. Even my mother and father, who told me it was too late, loved the baby and said it was the best thing I ever did. And my children? They loved the baby and showed him off whenever they could.

From time to time, I would pass maternity shops. I never went into one, not because of discomfort but because I had no need to wear maternity clothes. I had pretty clothes, jackets, dresses, and pants with tops that looked good on me before I became pregnant and that still looked good on me after I became pregnant. I did not carry large, and even when I finally showed, it was just a round ball in front of me that you could hardly see when I wore a jacket. When I was younger, I gained weight all over and looked swollen. I was nauseous and self-conscious. It felt different this time. It felt better.

But even though I never had need to go into one of those shops, my grown daughter, not I, was uncomfortable when we passed one. Embarrassed, she asked me either not to go in, or to go in with her so she could say that she was the one who was pregnant. I agreed not to go in, but she did not need to be embarrassed. I, for one, was proud to be toppling people's expectations.

I loved being pregnant. I felt euphoric. My body was changing, with life inside it; what, I thought, could be more important? People started to ask me questions when they realized I was pregnant again, despite already having two kids in their twenties:

"Is this your second marriage?"

"Can you handle it?"

"Did you have a career first?"

When I was pregnant in my twenties, and busy putting my husband through law school, the answer to that last question would have been very different. But this time, I had a PhD under my belt and had built an edifying career. I knew who I was and what I wanted. Besides, people's questions no longer concerned me.

GETTING EASIER

Ari was delivered by C-section. I had picked the day for delivery, received a small bikini cut, and went home with a baby. I did not have to go through the horrendous contractions, being in a delivery room, delivering without my husband, and being in horrible pain without any medication—all things that happened when I had given birth to my son twenty-seven years earlier. Back then, my husband was not even allowed into the delivery room. I had to lie flat on my back in order to deliver, and no medication was given.

I shouldn't have been so surprised that it was easier to give birth at fifty-three than it had been at twenty-seven. I had assumed it would be harder. But contrary to what most people think, doctors told me, the procedure itself—not one's age—is what determines how easy or hard a delivery will be.

I quickly rushed my children in to see their newborn brother. I did not have any need for them to be concerned about my well-being. I was thrilled, just as I knew I would be all along.

Although there is a wide age gap, my older children never doubted that they had a younger brother. They did not play the parent role.

Having a baby even at age forty was pretty revolutionary during my mother's time. Before my mother passed away at eighty-seven, she had hinted that, after getting pregnant at forty-three, she had miscarried on purpose by washing the floors on her hands and knees, so strong was her fear of deviating from normal motherhood expectations. I know that it won't be long before it's no longer considered revolutionary to have a baby when you're older than fifty. Even in the decade after Ari was born, it had become far less astounding.

As time goes on and we see even more fertility options become available, I do not think pregnancy after fifty, or even after sixty, will be so unusual. Women's groups for older mothers will consist of women over fifty and will reflect a new way of looking at motherhood and relationships. Starting over is a concept that we have accepted at this age. Now, motherhood will be part of that concept.

I am part of a very small but growing population giving birth later in life, thanks to technological advances in fertility (and a lot of determination). But my generation of women has always been on the cutting edge of change. We were the first to have real careers, demand equality in our relationships, and demand equal pay. We could be feminine and assertive at the same time. Now, we are making newer changes through the years. In some small way, I hope that we are redefining age and making a path for others to follow.

5

How Life Began Again (And Again) at Sixty

I FIRST EMBARKED ON MY QUEST TO BECOME A MOTHER yet again when Ari was a toddler, in hope that he would have someone to play with. *A brother or sister would be perfect,* I would think, fantasizing about siblings playing together.

At first I thought of adoption, and then of in vitro fertilization and surrogacy. More than three years passed between the moment I decided I wanted to try for kids and the time we took the trip that would end in my pregnancy, so that by the time Ari actually got those siblings, he was seven years old.

Sometimes things work out in ways we would never have expected. When I embarked on a journey to have another child when I was already in my late fifties, I was certain I wanted it to happen but could not clearly see *how* it would happen. The circumstances that set my record-breaking pregnancy in motion involved rain—lots and lots of rain—a cruise ship, and even Donald Trump.

DONALD TRUMP AND THE BABY BUMP

Shortly before I became pregnant, my whole family went on a cruise together. We had been looking forward to a tranquil, relaxing vacation. But the seas were much rougher than expected.

"Look at the beautiful waves," I had said at first. "This is not Disneyland," someone offered as a reality check as we watched the sea rise higher and higher.

And indeed, this was serious. Seawater was spilling over the sides of the ship. I looked around and saw that the large dining room of the cruise ship was emptying out. People were running, dishes were falling and I could hardly walk to my cabin, even when I took my shoes off.

Our family stayed in our adjoining two cabins for three long days. When I lay in bed at night, I felt like I had vertigo. On top of the turbulence, there was some weird talk that the captain of this cruise ship was trying to turn back to shore for a media shoot for Donald Trump. Later, I would be bumped off of the Oprah show for Trump, who in a funny twist of fate may have been the indirect cause of that baby bump in the first place.

Instead of doing those fun cruise activities I had been counting on, I read a magazine about in vitro fertilization and how the experience was cheaper for older mothers in certain parts of Africa. According to the article, in Africa the procedure would cost three thousand dollars, rather than the thirty thousand I would have to pay for IVF in New Jersey or New York. *Interesting*, I thought, and I tucked the article into my purse for future reading.

Once safely back in New Jersey (yes, we survived that cruise), I continued to think about yet another child, a sibling for Ari. Adoption seemed a more realistic option than IVF. Plus, while Jaeson and Alana looked askance at my idea about getting pregnant again, they were more open to the idea of adopting a child.

So I planned to adopt. Wheels were set in motion. I found an agency and followed all their instructions, taking fingerprints of me, my husband, and our children. It was just a matter of time before the adoption could happen, and I was ready. But I kept looking back at that article I had taken from the cruise that almost killed us.

I did more research and found that the article was right: older prospective mothers can get in vitro treatments much less expensively overseas. And when I heard about some bad outcomes from people who had adopted, I was even more intrigued by the possibility of IVF overseas.

But just because IVF options were available, there was of course no guarantee that they would succeed. Even if I were to undergo the treatment, I assumed I'd have to return home and proceed with adoption. I was fifty-six at the time, one year older than what one doctor had told me was the cutoff date for in vitro treatment. (I would later learn that other doctors didn't believe in such a cut-off age.)

I showed the article to Ken. "I am too old," I said. "But the price is right."

"No," he replied. "You are not too old. You're young for your years, so we'll try it."

IT HAPPENED IN AFRICA

Even though time was important, it took us three years to finally go to Africa. Jaeson and Alana were sure that I would not get pregnant. "Have fun," they said, confident that I would be forced to go forward with adoption, not pregnancy.

Shortly after we made the plane and hotel reservations, my mother got very sick, which made me cautious about taking such a big trip. But not only did my husband want to avoid losing our plane fare, he also said that despite the distance, I would be able to talk with my mother every day and that my brother would be available to take care of her. We got the support of Ari's school principal and embarked on our two-week trip.

Two weeks before, I had gotten progesterone injections, to enhance the possibility that the eggs I'd have implanted would be viable. I had frozen my own eggs. When we arrived at the fertility clinic, I thought the people there would share my concern about the long plane trip. But they had no problem with it. Many people from America visited them, they assured me, and they did not see it as a big deal.

Although the trip had its hiccups, including a rough safari and an even rougher helicopter ride, we came home from it elated. Everyone was happy . . . until some news came to light: in a weirdly matter-of-fact voice, an administrator from the clinic told me some shocking news.

I was pregnant. The IVF treatment in Africa had worked.

We shared the news with our children. That's when I started to hear that I was being selfish. My daughter said I was too old. My son said it was *his* turn, time for me to step back and make room for the next generation.

Even though I loved my children dearly, I had a response to their criticism—a refrain that had been running through my head from a young age. Now it was time to stand up for what I wanted: "No. No, no," I said.

My options are my own. There is no one to define where I need to be. Children, career, location, relationship—they are now all choices. I did not realize this when I was younger, nor did my parents have access to the huge amount of personal freedom that is at our fingertips today. Pleasing others and putting our desires aside is the thing of the past. But doing what we want, joyfully, and being there for ourselves so that we can be authentically present for others too? That is, in my opinion, the wisest thing anyone can possibly do.

THE DOCTORS

Even the seemingly simple act of confirming my pregnancy was not so easy.

Doctor Number One put the probe right on my pelvic area and pressed really hard. "Aren't you going to damage the fetus?" I asked. "No," he said. "It's too small to be affected."

That night, I bled, so I called him. He said I was probably miscarrying, and he asked me to come in for a blood test so we could find out. I couldn't believe how cavalier he was. Here I was, back from a trip to Africa, sixty years old, and he's asking me to come in for a blood test. Ho-hum. That day, I lay on the couch at home and did not move. I ended up on that couch for five days while my husband tended to me.

I never went back to that doctor and I didn't pay him either.

Doctor Number Two reported that I was indeed pregnant. And he told me a lot more than that. As he looked at an ultrasound screen, he said he saw a foot—and then another one. "Another foot?" I asked. "Another hand?" No, he said, another baby. "What did you just say? Another baby?" And with that, Ken and I started crying. As we walked out of the office, the nurses all congratulated us. We were ecstatic, and at that point I knew more than ever that I wanted the children.

The doctor talked to us for two hours while he had a waiting room full of people. They all smiled at us as we walked out. Although I liked this doctor a lot, my husband didn't. He was very troubled by the prospect, raised by the doctor himself, that we might have to rely on his colleagues and not be guaranteed to deal only with him. He might be called away to deal with one of his VIP patients, including Catherine Zeta-Jones. That reservation led to us needing to find another doctor.

Emotionally, I felt fragile and conflicted this time. My mother was still ill, and I felt pulled in two directions; I wanted to take care of her, and my mind and heart were with her, but at the same time I was immersed in this pregnancy. Around my husband I was acting elated about the twins, while I was crying on the inside for my mother. Not really taking care of my own needs and yet again trying to make my husband happy, I refused to cry on the outside or show my husband how worried I was about my mother.

Soon I met Doctor Number Three, Abdulla Al-Khan.

"*How* old did you say you are?" he asked. "Let's look at the sonogram and see for ourselves what is going on inside you." He said he could not believe that a sixty-year-old woman could be pregnant, but here I was.

Ken had some reservations. The day after my first appointment, he emailed the doctor to say that we could no longer see him because he is Muslim and we are Jewish. But I didn't feel that way at all. I begged the doctor to overlook my husband's reaction, insisted that *I* am the patient, and told him that I would even name a child after him if he went ahead. After meeting with a panel of other doctors, Dr. Al-Khan agreed to work with me.

Dr. Al-Khan was a gift. He was compassionate and involved, and I looked forward to seeing him. The pregnancy was uneventful. And he was wonderfully attentive to me. He gave me a manicure and pedicure while I was in the hospital (telling me that he did that for all his patients), and, best of all, he made me the most delicious crushed-almond cookies after I gave birth. Later, he would even come to my sons' bris. My husband, by this time over his initial hesitation, had come to love him so much that he wanted him as a son-in-law.

As I got off the elevator for one of my appointments at the hospital in Hackensack, New Jersey, another doctor, the hospital's obstetrics head, kissed me on both cheeks. Alas, I always felt that *that* doctor saw me as a novelty and was eyeing the publicity potential after he invited me into his office and asked whether I would be willing to reveal my age to the world.

I had to think about that. Dr. Al-Khan had asked me to tell no one my age. Besides, all the nurses at the hospital were telling me I looked like I was forty, so I figured that I'd keep stretching the truth to anyone who asked. But this doctor said that I would make a difference to the women of the world if I revealed that I was really giving birth at *sixty,* an age that struck a nerve with so many people.

All my life, I had lied about my age. But hearing that remark made me understand the significance of my journey. I let my doctor alert the media. Suddenly the switch boards were overrun with messages for me from the press around the country and people who claimed they knew me. They hired an extra operator for me and installed guards at my door night and day who escorted me everywhere I went. Suddenly, when I had something to say, people were listening attentively.

PARENTHOOD GOT EASIER

When I was pregnant at fifty-three, I worried about what people would think of my decision. I also worried about whether I had the energy to take this on. It turns out that I need not have worried; the birth went well, and I didn't feel any less energetic running after Ari than I had running after Jaeson or Alana. And then, when Jaret and Josh came along, I felt up to the task of caring for them.

I feel—and my husband has expressed a similar feeling!—that my energy level has been enhanced by the twins. With motherhood, this time around, having been so badly wanted and so painstakingly pursued, we do not take them for granted. We celebrate their lives and plan excitedly for the future.

People may doubt this, and other older mothers' experiences may be different. But I can only share my own experience. It's possible that some maternal instinct kicked in and my body and mind have become energized by the task of motherhood. And in this way, I don't think I am unique. Often I see women in their forties with children, and they appear more vibrant, somehow bouncier, than mothers who were in their thirties.

When I was in my fifties, being perceived as old should have been furthest from my mind. After all, now that I'm in my sixties and a mother of twins, I've been written off as "old" by people around the world. And it doesn't bother me. I focus on the present. I focus on how *I* feel.

When I was a younger mother, I did not relish the important aspects of childhood as much as I do now. I was fortunate to have two beautiful children who delighted me, yet I was not as prepared to be as responsible as I was when I was older. Perhaps it did not feel as natural or as effortless to me then as it does now.

The so-called sacrifices that come with motherhood—losing sleep, wiping noses, feeling like a glorified (or unglorified) chauffeur—came more easily to me in my fifties than they did in my thirties. And in my sixties, despite the naysayers who said I'd be winded by playing tag with Josh and Jaret, these "sacrifices" feel easier than ever. They say being a grandmother is more exciting than having your own children. But I wonder if it's not the later age that has a great deal to do with the appreciation of a newborn baby.

The best part: my husband and I *take turns* nurturing them. In the past, my husband bowed to the then-traditional norms that said I should handle all childcare. Admittedly I still do more than half of it. But his attitude has changed with the times, and he now embraces his nurturing side more than ever before.

And my older children, once aghast at my decision to give birth at sixty, can't stop showing the twins off to everyone they see.

If you're asking yourself whether you should give birth at an older-than-usual age, I cannot say whether you should or should not follow in my footsteps. But if you are wondering whether you *can* start something new, regardless of how "old" society says you are? In my view, you already know the answer.

I am more excited by life than ever before. And that excitement—about my new view on life, and about my twins—has only grown since I turned sixty.

HARDSHIPS

My experience was not all sunshine and roses, of course. We left for Africa at a terrible time; my mother was very ill, and while she was away the doctors treated her with a blood thinner.

My son was so angry that I went to Africa at such a bad time that he refused to speak to me. I was sorry I went. I felt a little resentful of my husband, as he had insisted that we go after he had already purchased the tickets, even though I was worried about my ailing mother. To this day, in dark moments, I sometimes think: *I don't know if my husband realizes what I did for him. I left my mother who I loved dearly, left my son and daughter whom I loved dearly, and sacrificed my comfort with injections in order to make him happy.* (He wanted this addition to the family badly, just like I did.) In Africa, every time I called my mother, Ken would spy on me and say, "We are not calling your mother again." I was livid.

My mother started throwing up blood. She was taken from a rehab center to the hospital, and because she was eighty-seven and on Medicare they would only treat her for three months in intensive care. She suffered badly and died of internal bleeding five months before the twins were born. Her last words in Yiddish were, "I'm hungry."

When we learned that we were having twins, and everyone was happy and celebrating, I was crushed about losing my mother. I knew that my mother had needed me with her, to save her life. I knew I should have been with her, and felt caught between devotion to my mother and devotion to my husband. My heart was crying out for her while I felt trapped in what was for me an empty celebration.

The care my mother received in the hospital was sloppy and negligent. They gave her the wrong medicine and misdiagnosed her, and the doctor from the rehab center was uncommunicative. I found out later that my uncle also died from an overdose of blood thinner from the same center. I believed that if I had been there rather than in Africa, I could have prevented all this from happening.

My mother and I were very close, especially toward the end of her life. We enjoyed being together even if we were doing nothing. One of my fondest memories was being in the hospital, watching television together and sleeping in a chair overnight so I could see she was all right. She had set out for rehab with special clothes in order to socialize with the other women but she ended up dying instead.

My relationship with my son Jaeson suffered, too; he felt betrayed, like I had chosen to focus on getting pregnant over my mother. Yet my husband was never questioned. Thankfully, Jaeson and I reconciled and are now closer than ever. Today his children play with my children and he comes over whenever he wants.

My family has always felt very interconnected; if one of us is not all right, then we are all affected.

After I had the twins, my life changed forever. Not because of the twins, not because of my age, but because I had revealed my age. Little did I know that I started something of a revolution. All I had done was have babies through in vitro fertilization. As it was for many women, it was uneventful for me. But unlike many women, I told my true age.

This made me feel very vulnerable. We're used to asking questions like, *Will you think I look old? Will you have thought I was younger?* Either way, revealing one's true age brings up a feeling of great insecurity for many of us.

Not until I had my twins did I see that there was a need to adjust this attitude. Although I ultimately got a lot of negative feedback for having children at sixty, being older is nothing to be ashamed of.

So many studies have shown that people who feel younger live longer. That was going to be me, I decided. I am not some flighty person; I am a professional who has done a lot of research on women, success, and, now, age. What happened to me will be more and more acceptable as time goes on. I keep reminding myself that when Ari was born, I was fifty-three, which was shocking at the time. In the years since, it has become much less shocking. I was the oldest mother of twins in the United States. But was I the only mom who could have also been called "granny?" I doubt it.

Although people were quick to call me "old," "selfish," a "grannymom," and even a crazy lady, I was past the point in life where I would let people's words crush me. The important thing, I realized, it was not how the world represented my age but how I represented my age to the world.

I accepted many of the publicity invitations that rolled in. With the help of my two adult children, my very proud husband, and my seven-year-old son, I juggled changing diapers and putting infants to sleep with furtive drives into New York. I appeared on *20/20*, *Entertainment Tonight*, and countless network shows. I said "yes" to interviews by the *Daily Mail* and *USA Today*. The questions people asked me were not always friendly, but I shared my story openly and without hesitation.

As people kept asking me questions about what it meant to get older, I thought hard about what that meant to me. Beyond reaching into my personal life and my family's past, I thought about the research I had carried out and the clients I had seen as a psychotherapist. I hope my *new* view on what it means to be a mother, a partner, and to reinvent ourselves—as explored in the following chapters—will empower you right now and far into the future.

After all, people could criticize me all they wanted for being old and starting something new, but I know the truth: life can begin at any age.

PART II

LIFE BEGINS AT ANY AGE:
MY NEW VIEWS

6

Write Your Own Fairy Tale

IN PART I OF THIS BOOK, I SHARED WITH YOU THE STORY OF MY PAST and explained how my decisions had consistently been affected by external pressures: my parents' protective restrictions, my peers' looking askance when I didn't spend every single moment with my children due to pursuing my education and then a career, my husband's expectations that I should be a housewife and was not to be taken seriously. . . . I tried and I tried and I tried some more to satisfy people's desires while tuning in so strongly to others' expectations that I felt at my *own* core a mysterious emptiness.

I took that palpable sense seriously, and asked "Is this it?" I spent years upon years researching women's happiness before carrying out deep analysis and then applied my findings to real case studies, as I had observed them in my psychotherapeutic practice. What emerged was, in my view, some highly practical insight into how women can make themselves happy in the context of their families. In the following pages, I hope to address that nagging, vexing voice inside that implored, "Is this it?" by explaining how "this" did not have to be "it." Some of the advice in this chapter was consistent with how I acted, while I *wish* I had followed other pieces of advice. I am not claiming to know everything about marriage, motherhood, age, and how to be happy inside and out-side the home. But I hope that, in sharing my views, I can give you some company in navigating all of these things as well as some reassurance that, whatever your age, *you* are vital, capable and ready to enjoy your life right this very minute.

DON'T GET SWEPT OFF YOUR FEET

My marriage and all the big decisions that were part of it have never been smooth and easy. Ken and I might end up in similar places, but the road leading there has usually been very bumpy. We have different styles and approaches to many different things. When I was younger, I wanted a family much more than he did. Even now, when we each give the twins something they need, we do it differently. I do a lot of the work of parenting while Ken plays with the kids more.

I could have taken that trip to Africa, or chosen some other option, earlier.

Remember how, as a young mother, I sent out those surveys? When my young kids and my husband were asleep, I enlisted the statistician to work his magic. As I'd so dearly hoped, the survey results shed light on the relationships between marriage, work, and happiness.

* * *

As years went by, and I kept seeing patients in my home office in Saddle River, New Jersey, lots of different people came through the door. In this suburban environment, many of my clients were women who wanted to improve their home lives. Often they were on the brink of divorce and wanted to save their marriages.

Basically I learned that being happily coupled up in the suburbs is not, for most women, a recipe for automatic bliss.

Instead, it is important to have an identity outside of the home. Freezing eggs, doing IVF, and generally undergoing motherhood later in life has a wealth of positive effects for women, whether they are single or in a relationship. In the following pages, I will make the case for why cultivating an independent identity makes for a better home life. Often this "independent identity" takes the form of a career. Women who expect to be swept off their feet in some kind of fairy tale, rather than creating something for themselves, are for the most part setting themselves up for unhappiness. Which is to say: if you want to put off motherhood and have a way to do so, and feel that it is the right decision for you, I highly recommend it.

MARRIAGE AND HAPPINESS: THE BASICS

As I continued to see patients, read, study, and think about my own situation, some interesting conclusions emerged.

The first is that you have to know yourself in order to meet someone healthy. Another is that you should reassess your life every five years in order to make changes.

In addition . . .

- When women have a career and a family, they are often called "selfish."
- Women often regard love as everything. For men, love is often just one part of their identities.
- Midlife crises do not have to happen. They probably won't—if we understand our needs and find a way to express them. (Remember my mother's unspoken messages, and the sense of conflictedness they stirred up in me?) If we don't, though, we are likely to succumb—and at any age.
- Divorce can be either good or bad, but no matter what happens it does not need to get ugly. It depends on how both parties handle it. After a divorce, men often look to have a relationship because they need to fill a part of themselves that is missing. Women, though, seek fulfillment on their own.

Many of my female clients are incredibly stressed out. Why are so many women stressed? In my view, it's because we're in the midst of conflict. In the 1950s, being a full-time mother was the thing to do, but women doing it were often depressed. In later years, having a career and working outside the home became the women's revolution; women were indeed less depressed, but they were left exhausted.

In the twenty-first century, women feel they are missing a vital part of themselves by not staying home with the children. Yet they find their husbands are not giving them the right treatment, and their relationships suffer.

My research showed that women who have careers have better relationships with their family and husbands. The answer to the age-old question of whether to have a career or stay home with the children is to do both. Children will thrive by seeing a mother who is fulfilled. The woman's relationship with her husband is equal and provides greater respect for the woman's ideas. The choice of whether to have a career or family during the woman's revolution is over. Having both is the best way to happiness.

Because women no longer need to get married for security, they instead marry men who have the qualities they are seeking. This puts a man in the same role as the woman. Is he in good shape? Is he smart, successful, good-looking, nurturing? Women are looking for more, and men are providing more. A lot has changed since the women's revolution, but then again a lot has not. As long as women are seen as objects, women will be restrained from being looked at as individuals, no matter what their age.

When women are accomplished and empowered, they have more power to make decisions in and outside a relationship. No longer do they need to be competitive with other women to prove themselves. They know who they are. Women with less power are more likely to lie about their age because they are more prone to find their identity through other people.

The reasons for marrying are changing. These reasons make women less dependent on the man. They no longer have to fear abandonment, double standards, or have a submissive role in the relationship. Women who make more money are disinclined to marry; they are not willing to exchange independence for dependence. They are not looking for a provider—in other words, a Prince Charming who will automatically create a "happily ever after" and therefore do not feel the same pressure to marry.

7

Throw "Normal" Out the Window

THE WORLD WAS SHOCKED WHEN I HAD BABIES AT sixty; it just wasn't "normal," many said. But what shocked *me* more was how the world looked at my age. People told me I was old, even though I felt better than I ever had in my life.

Thanks to the attention that my unusual story garnered, I started hearing from other women. One after the other, they showed me that I may not have been so abnormal after all. On a given week there would be, for instance, a fifty-two-year-old woman in the school parking lot who told me her late-in-life pregnancy story as I dropped Josh and Jaret off for the day, and then a friend who told me she had decided to pursue IVF in her forties because I had "given her permission to live her life." (Of course, no one needs permission to live their life; the fact that we speak in these terms highlights the extent to which women push their needs to the back burner, conditioned to do so at nearly every stage.)

When I first made the talk show rounds, women from Dubai, Germany, Japan, and London called and emailed me. Often they were professionals who had taken the time to develop their careers before considering children. More and more women were empowered to cultivate lives *outside* of the home before turning their thoughts to engagement rings and dirty diapers . . . a decision that my research showed would have positive ripple effects *inside* the home, too. My mother did not have this option, and when I was a young mother I did not feel empowered to take it either. From where I am standing, the future looks very bright for all of us to who choose later-in-life pregnancy, now that it is an option.

If we go down that particular "abnormal" path, it turns out, we are not alone. In addition to the thousands of non-famous women who choose motherhood at forty plus, an array of celebrities have done it.

For instance . . .

- Geena Davis gave birth to Alizeh at forty-six and had twin boys Kian and Kaiis two years later.
- The British actress Patricia Hodge had Alexander at forty-two and Edward at forty-five.
- Jennifer Beals gave birth to her first child, a daughter, at forty-two.

- Salma Hayek gave birth to daughter Valentina at forty-one.
- Emma Thompson had her daughter Gaia at forty.
- Helen Fielding had her son Dashiell at forty-five and a daughter at forty-eight.
- Annie Leibovitz gave birth to her daughter Sarah at fifty-one. Her twins Susan and Samuelle were born to a surrogate mother four years later.
- Courteney Cox gave birth to Coco two days before her fortieth birthday.
- Halle Berry famously became pregnant at forty-six.

AGE IS CHANGING

Along with all the new options that exist, the concept of age is changing—and the world needs to catch up.

People are living longer. The United States Census Bureau reports that the senior age group will triple by 2050. It's essential that older people, especially women, learn to view their later decades as opportunities to contribute to society. And the younger people, too, need to recognize the same thing. One out of nine baby-boomers will reach age ninety. Optimism, being active, and having fun all help. We have raised life expectancy to 78.2 years, according to the United Nations Population Division. (Japan ranks on top with a life expectancy of 82.6 years.) The average person who turned sixty-five can expect to live to almost eighty-four. Death rates are at an all-time low, while life expectancy is at an all-time high according to the Centers for Disease Control and Prevention.

First, we need to address the gender issues surrounding the concept of age. When a man tells his age, he is judged by what he does. Equality with age needs to be addressed. No one asked my husband how old he was. Yet men typically live eight years less than women. My neighbor, a fifty-three-year-old man, has school-age children and no one bats an eye. But if he were a woman, people might be asking questions like "Aren't you a little old for that?"

In a way, age equality is our last frontier. According to many, men having babies when they are older are virile, while women having babies when they are older are "crazy." Who made these rules? Fighting for myself with my in-laws, husband, and society, I have always fought to break rules where I thought they should be broken.

A stranger on the steps of the New York Public Library once told me, "You will make a difference one day." I hope I am making a difference to women by showing them life is not over after a certain age. Life is different and much better. Don't listen to what society is saying; just listen to yourself. The authority out there is not necessarily there for your best interest.

In fact, as you get older you come to understand that the only real authority in life is yourself.

THE AUTHORITY IS YOU

Google me and you will see all the hate mail. Women long ago had children into their fifties. But I struck a nerve. The age of sixty is that nerve. I think the age of forty used to hit that nerve. My mother confided in me that at forty-three she miscarried, apparently on purpose because she was ashamed.

Society has not yet caught up with what is actually happening. Women are tiptoeing into change—changing their status, changing their careers, changing their relationships.

Why now? Because the baby-boomers have always had to make changes. The early feminists, like Betty Friedan and Gloria Steinem, led the way by redefining relationships and careers, and now I like to think that I am leading the way with age.

But unlike the militant times of the past, we do not have to be aggressive. Just honest. Hillary Clinton is probably today's highest-profile woman, but is she being heard? Her aggressive personality has often worked against her. But during her younger years, women had to be aggressive to be heard. The choice was either to be militant or to take a back seat and be controlled. That is no longer the case.

As long as there is a double standard for age, women will not tell their age for fear of being judged. But by whom? By both men and other women. If we let *them* have the final answer, then we will have to live with *their* answer, not ours. Their answer seems to benefit them. Women still have a reason to be kept down. They are still made to feel inferior. Age is the reason. It's the last taboo. We need to tell the truth so no one can intimidate us. We need to see that it is okay to speak out and to pursue what we want at forty, fifty, sixty, or older. No one should tell us not to do something because, for someone our age, it is not "normal."

We were once told that it was not okay to have a career or to have equality in relationships. But we fought against that. Yet that all seems so passé today. Someday, ageism, too, will be passé, but not yet. A woman at sixty and a man at sixty conjure up different images. Why? Who is making these rules? We need to stand up for older mothers, older women, and younger men, younger lifestyles, and say it's okay. We might as well understand and accept that that's what is now happening.

On one hand, I hated being pigeonholed and getting the message, everywhere I turned, that there were things I *could* do and things I *couldn't* do. Certain behavior was expected of me. They were roiling times, as a woman's place in society was being reexamined and redefined. Different women had different priorities. Although the idea that I was no longer being held to a strict timetable for relationships, career, and marriage was wonderful, I bristled constantly at the age discrimination I saw around me. And it would be decades before I acted on it in a way that got the world's attention: having babies at age sixty.

It keeps coming back to aging. That's always the main issue for a woman. Consider the whole issue of middle age, which society believes begins in the late thirties or so. But middle age is the best time for both your body and your mind. It has come to mean so much more than just the midpoint of some average lifespan.

How could people say I was middle-aged? I was told that I looked better, and I know that I felt better, than I ever had in my life. But I kept silent because no one wanted to hear that. Will I still feel better as I get older?

Will I still look and feel better than ever? It didn't really matter, because I was no longer looking for anyone to tell me that it was okay. I am no longer letting others take away my power.

When I was twenty, I was told it was time to get married, so I did, at age twenty-two.

When I was in my early twenties, I was told that pretty girls were a dime a dozen and that I'd better get a career.

When I was twenty-six, after supporting my husband through law school, I was told that I'd better have children or people would think there was something wrong with me, so I did.

When I was thirty, I was told I was not a young girl any longer, that I was a woman, as if there was something wrong with being a woman.

When I was thirty-five, I was told I was middle-aged, which was, to listen to some jealous women, the only reason I was accepted into Columbia Graduate School.

When I was forty, I saw a cutesy coffee mug in a drugstore. The mug said I was over the hill.

When I was forty-five, I was told I had jowls.

When I was fifty, I was told I was not a spring chicken anymore.

When I was sixty, the world told me I was old and that it was someone else's turn.

But in the wake of all that criticism, and after years upon years of being told how I should feel, I finally realized that it was not how the world saw me but how I saw myself that made the difference. In short, I said, *Enough already! When will it be my turn?* I realized I would have to take my own sensibilities to the grave if I did not stop this now. No one could tell me that I was too old to handle anything; no one could tell me what to do at all.

Compare for yourself. See whether you see age the same way I do:

Age	The traditional way	The new way
20s	Marriage and family	Explore the world, develop yourself and a career
30s	Raise a family	Have a career and/or relationship and/or children
40s	Peak of career	May develop a relationship; have children and career
50s	Grandchildren	Children and/or grandchildren
60s	Retire	New options

The message we project is the message we get back. Age is in the mind. Feeling young is available for any age. Don't give in to societal pressures. It is not good for your health.

8

Take Yet Another Risk

Bᴇᴄᴀᴜsᴇ ᴏꜰ ᴛʜᴇ ᴍᴇssᴀɢᴇs ᴀʙᴏᴜᴛ ᴀɢᴇ ᴛᴏ ᴡʜɪᴄʜ ᴡᴇ are subjected throughout life, we sometimes feel too old to take risks—even when that is far from being the case. We turn forty (which is young) and suddenly panic: *What are our plans? Who have we become? Do we have to retire from life? What do we do with all our resources?*

And as women, we also have to ask ourselves: *Why are we being told to hide ourselves away?*

DISCRIMINATION
Discrimination in any form is ugly, and I have always been especially sensitive to it. Remember that my parents were survivors of a Siberian labor camp, where

they were sent during World War II, essentially for being Jewish; thankfully, they were not murdered during the Holocaust. Their lives before I was born, as far as I understand it, were all about survival. My thinking about age, pregnancy, feminism — well, my thinking about everything in my life — was shaped by them, especially by what they endured. As immigrants, as so many in our country are, they worked hard for everything they had. While I was dealing with cameras in my face after giving birth at sixty, I thought about my parents dodging bullets as they fled Poland and left their parents behind.

At times I thought, *If my mother could have children after such a torturous existence then who am I to have the spotlight right now?* It seemed obvious to me that my parents came first. After all, they had gone through hell and back to survive with their family. Now I needed to take care of them.

In addition to coming to America with four children and the emotional scars of the War, they had to deal with numerous misunderstandings, ignorance, and a humongous cultural gap. They were, after all, foreigners in a strange new world. They put their lives on the line to protect their family during the Holocaust.

So traumatic was my father's wartime experience that he didn't let any tears flow until I took out that tape recorder in my twenties. And through his life in various parts of the United States, he continued to experience hardships in the form of anti-Semitism. I vividly remember sitting in a car with my parents in Brooklyn one day when a group of teenagers passed by and snickered at them and called them names. Adrenaline was flowing in every part of my body when I shouted at them, "You get back here and apologize." My father, who never really considered his own safety, had saved a few people in Europe during the war, and I guess that served as an example to me. These kids could have been carrying guns or knives, but they turned around, came back, and apologized instead.

I would not tolerate any discrimination against them. I always stood up for them, and their happiness was mine. So I certainly wasn't going to tolerate any discrimination against myself.

Age discrimination may not manifest itself as brutally as anti-Semitism during World War II or harassment of immigrants, but it is a form of discrimination nonetheless. In a way, it is the last taboo. It may not be explicit, but it still manifests itself.

As I write this on January 5th of this year, actress Dakota Johnson is telling *British Vogue* that ageism is "brutal" in Hollywood. "Why isn't my mother in the movies? She's an extraordinary actress. Why isn't my grandmother in the movies?" she asked. Her mother is Melanie Griffith, her grandmother Tippi Hedren. What a waste of talent.

As we get older we are more assertive, and we have our own minds more than ever, but we are told to be passive instead of taking risks. There's so much information that needs to be shared but that is stored away instead. The media, advertising, fashion still don't take full advantage of what women have to offer. We have financial resources, style, and passion. But where is our platform for all of this? Turn on a television show and see how many people over sixty are out there, sharing their stories. Where are we?

Women are still classified by what is "appropriate" for their age. Men are not. Powerful, famous men are not questioned about their fatherhood. No one asked my husband, who happens to be a few years older than I, how old he was when his twin sons were born.

Age discrimination may be the last frontier of the feminist movement that began in the 1960s. I am no Gloria Steinem (who by the way has expressed regret about not having children). But I fought having to be either independent or domesticated and I am fighting to make a difference to the world through my research, not by having babies.

When it comes to age discrimination against women, we still have a long way to go. Even though people might laugh at us or imply that we should hide ourselves away, we need to step out of the shadows and take the risks that come with speaking out—demonstrating, of course, how wise, wonderful, visible, and vital we all can be.

9

Demand Respect— or a Divorce

IN MY MOTHER'S GENERATION, DIVORCE WAS NOT A respectable option. Among the clients that I counsel today, I find that increasingly it can be a wise choice when one person in the relationship is not getting the respect they deserve, no matter how much they express themselves and assert their needs. In the case histories below, women who have not been able to fulfill themselves because of their husband's attitudes often sought divorce in order to regain their individuality.

The social pressure of the late 1980s and women's wish to work, combined with their husbands' attitudes, financial situation, age, and number of children, are some of the factors that have played an important force in women's motivation for achievement. Women who grew up in the 1930s, 1940s, and 1950s had less conflicting role models than did those who grew up in the 1960s. That's because women in the 1960s were simultaneously influenced by the values of their own traditional mothers and by the feminist movement. Previously, women had gained their satisfactions by identifying with their husbands' professional roles.

A woman could easily leave her husband for a new man, but then she would be just another statistic. Instead, she can have the same husband and a new relationship. Consider Janet:

Janet was miserable and realized that every time she was in a relationship, she gave up her own identity. Janet felt angry with her husband, Ted, for taking advantage of her. She was ready to leave him and start a relationship with someone else. But because she had two children, Janet decided to stay. What she learned was that her husband reacted to her need to give, so he expected her to give more than should be expected.

During their seven years of marriage, he made his demands, and she reacted favorably and reluctantly at the same time. He wanted her home before him. If he did not like her friends, she would have to get rid of them. Janet decided to change her identity within her relationship. She told Ted she needed to be independent, make her own friends, choose her own schedule, and be her own person. This was difficult for Ted, as he felt threatened and insecure, but he did not want to lose Janet. Slowly, Ted was able to enjoy Janet's differences in friends and started to

As a child, I spent most of my time
helping my mother around the house
...and dreaming of being on stage.

With my two sisters, my brother, and my parents at home in Cleveland, Ohio.

My parents, whose journey to the United States was fraught with danger.

On vacation in my twenties . . . pre-motherhood.

As I walked down the aisle, I wondered if I'd get the chance to fulfill my ambitions.

My sisters, Rachel and Goldie, by my side on my wedding day.

It was supposed to be the happiest day of my life.

Ken and me as newlyweds.

Embracing our first child.

With my first son, Jaeson, in my thirties.

As a mom of two in my early thirties, I was making everyone happy. Sometimes, though, my smile felt forced.

Ken and me with Alana.

A glamorous moment in my thirties.

Another happy memory from my early thirties. You can tell it's the 1980s here.

Another very eighties shot, this time with my daughter Alana.

Playing dress-up with Alana.

With my mother, who often kept her feelings inside as she catered to the family's needs.

As a new mom and a full-time student, I was always busy.

Dressed for work as a psychotherapist.

At my son Ari's *bris* ceremony, I was a
new mom again—at fifty-three.

Being the mother of a young teenager (and even younger twins) in my sixties often felt natural.

Josh and Jaret as newborns.

Me with my boys.

appreciate his wife for who she was. A new relationship resulted.

Women need to get what their primary relationship didn't give them: the missing part of themselves. They go to school, get careers, lose weight, and obtain a new perspective of themselves. They gain their own individuality and are much happier.

Donna felt dissatisfied. Her husband, Stan, was always critical of her. Although she made more money, he felt she made the wrong decisions. He wanted to save money for the future, but she wanted to enjoy life, buy pretty things for the home, remodel the house a little, and purchase clothing for the children.

He wanted to stay home on weekends and visit friends in the evening. She wanted to attend plays, go sightseeing, dine at the best restaurants, and travel. Whenever she felt she was doing something she liked, he found a reason to disagree with her. She was constantly being harassed by his argumentative ways. Her daughter, Jody, was even becoming more like her father, and this scared Donna.

Stan complained about his daughter's clothes, screamed at her when she didn't achieve certain grades, making her feel like a failure. In order to survive, Jody used her father's weapons of being critical, becoming difficult in order to retaliate. Was life supposed to be like being in prison? There was nothing she could enjoy with Stan. Even when they went on vacations, he found a reason to complain.

After several attempts at therapy, Donna finally decided to leave. She is now happier than ever. Her decisions are hers without any negative comments from an irritating and disagreeable spouse. Jody is calmer and does not have to put up a strong front to defend herself against her father. Stan needs to work on himself, finding out why he is so miserable and how to feel less inadequate in a marriage.

Men seek relationships. They look to fulfill a part of themselves that has not been fully developed. They are often more depressed.

Gary did not feel married and would often leave the family to go hunting or fishing. He had his own group of friends, and he related to them more than to his wife. When he did come back from his outdoor excursions, he acted indifferent in order to protect himself. His wife, Eleanor, was overwhelmed with motherhood and always complained because she felt alone and discontented.

Gary wasn't exactly proud of the fact that she did not take care of her appearance. Eleanor had become a complete slob by eating herself into an excessive weight category and not wearing any makeup to look a little presentable; Gary came to refer to her as "the old lady." This is how most men who have lost respect for their mates express their non-fondness of their wives. Disgusting, but true. Gary did not take time to realize her needs and that she needed more of him. His life belonged to him and no one else. Eventually he lost interest in her altogether. After the marriage went downhill, they argued about everything—from who was supposed to take the garbage out or who was supposed to contribute to household expenses to, worst of all, who was supposed to take care of their daughter.

After the divorce, Gary missed being in a relationship. He felt empty until finally finding someone whom he felt appreciated him. This time, he put more time into the relationship and helped it blossom. Because of this, he felt understood and started confiding more in his new partner. He was able to feel close and committed for the first time in his life. He was also proud of his wife and went out of his way to make her happy. He was a better father to the new family, and ended up liking himself more. He realized that a good marriage was better than being single. What he didn't realize was that if he had put the same commitment into the first marriage, it could have blossomed in the same way.

Eleanor had to come to the realization that if she didn't like herself, nobody else would like her, either. She had to learn to stand up for her beliefs and to set up the right kind of standards, from how she expects someone to take care of her child, to how she expects someone to take care of her. She developed a different side of herself. She realized that being single was better than being in a bad marriage. But looking for the right person who would be there for her was worth taking a second chance.

Divorce does not have to be the answer to reach any relationship goals. Two people who give each other the freedom of individuality during a marriage may not only prevent the pain of divorce but might also help with some issues that are necessary for a relationship. Why not improve the relationship with the person you are already with?

Most people, when asked, would rather work through their problems than leave the marriage. They are always aware of the damage that divorce can cause children.

Also, whatever problems they are having will often be repeated, so they may as well work on them right away.

A common dilemma after divorce is when one party realizes that he or she did not necessarily have to leave the relationship in order to fix the problems. Few people come to me for help and then get a divorce. Most come wanting to save their marriage, which is, of course, the No. 1 preference in their lives.

Does divorce have to get ugly? No. Getting along is far better. Go to a mediator or to a therapist, but just try to get along. The negative energy you are wasting on each other will sap away positive energy and misdirect you in your life. Consider this couple:

Laura and Steven realized that they were just much too different in every facet of life to continue living together. Laura was not going to permit Steven to have joint custody of their son. She felt Steven would be a bad influence on the boy and wanted to have a stronger role model for him. This was going to be the beginning of a long court battle. They both worked; Laura worked longer hours than her husband. Therefore, she needed to prove to the court she was able to handle the complete care of her son while at work.

In order to save years of battle and pain, Laura agreed to get along with Steven after the divorce and reluctantly agreed to joint custody. They each lived in the same neighborhood, and their son switched homes every two weeks. David was able to visit the same friends and go to the same school. Each parent was responsible for homework, activities, cooking, etc.

Steven had the opportunity to let his son see him as someone who is not a loser, as his wife saw him, but as someone who is strong and happy with himself as well as a good father. Steven did things with David, and David soon saw that his father's style was different. He learned to enjoy being more relaxed around his father rather than being tense about everything, as was his mother. David was given the opportunity to view his father in a positive light and to have the right role model after all.

If divorce does occur, there are ways to do it while minimizing the harassment. Couples often tend to distrust each other after divorce. This distrust and anger become the central theme. Instead of looking toward growth and the future, they often begin to look at each other with hate. They spend a great deal of time deciding how to get the other person back, forgetting that the divorce might be the answer for their happiness. They lose sight of the fact that each person is looking to live their way in a better manner.

This negative energy takes away from their ability to live their own lives. No matter how hard couples try not to, any children are often the scapegoats of their parents' misery, each parent playing against the other to be the child's favorite—by competing with or finding fault with the other. Both fail to realize that they both want what is best for the child, and that no divorce will work if they don't get along.

If they are not flexible with one another, what difference does the divorce custody mean? If one parent is sick, if one needs to go on a business trip, or if some other matter comes up requiring a parent to be someplace else, then they must be able to know that the other parent will work with them. The child or children will also see this working together and will be less stressed by the separation.

I have couples in my practice who are able to work together and are therefore able to listen to their children's needs. The children are able to say "I would like to go to mom's because I wath to play with my friend" or "I would like to go to dad's because I want to play baseball with him." When parents work together, the children will feel that they are not stuck in a situation where they have to make each parent happy but that instead they can express their own needs without worrying.

Therapy is often needed to help these couples get divorced in a friendly manner rather than a hostile one. Couples who agree with each other before and after the divorce settlement are happier than those who have obtained the so-called best settlement.

The best time to settle any differences is before you see a lawyer, because that is when the battle really begins. Avoiding the middlemen/middlewomen, the attorneys, from battling it out with each other hastens the dissolution of the marriage.

Alimony is a controversial topic because of women's careers and equal financial status. The conflict arises over whether each should be equally financially responsible or whether a woman who makes more money should she be required to support the husband. The conflict lies in the fact that no matter how much money a woman makes, she is often more involved with the children's well-being and, because of this, her time and efforts should be compensated.

Is it better to have a career first or children first? Used to be that women who had children first would feel the need to further themselves when the children entered school. The children of these women also decided to get educated and fulfill themselves first, before having a family. But today, with options more numerous, it seems that many people in their later years are more calm and family-oriented than in their earlier years, when they needed to succeed in their careers.

You can have children at a young age, then go to school to further your career intentions. But studies have found that mothers who have careers first and children later on in life were more satisfied. They fulfilled their needs to be productive as individuals and then had children when they were less driven to succeed outside the home and were more content.

So the answer to that very frequently asked question, which I address in many parts of this book — Should I have a career or children first? — is that in today's society the best thing for husband and wife is to have both together! In the past, the most common approach was having children, staying home, and delaying a career until the children left home. If you did work outside of the home, you were sometimes even called a bad mother.

But we are at a turning point on what is better for everyone. Women are choosing to stay home now more than ever. In the early days of the women's movement, when women had to assert themselves to be dealt with as equals, things often went the other way. Women no longer feel a need to have to prove themselves as much. But ironically, what is really best for everyone would be if the woman had a career of which she was proud.

My study has shown that children of these women are more confident and happier. My survey revealed that the relationship is better because the husband values his wife more. There is evidence in the literature that the happiest and healthiest women are those who have both a family and a career.

The fact is that not all women choose to have careers. Those who had mothers who were happy working outside the home tended to work outside the home themselves. But those women whose mothers were happy working as housewives were satisfied and content to be homemakers.

Women who had mothers who were not happy in the home had conflict, and these women often change their roles from housewife to a professional after marriage and after separating from their mothers. This change can bring on divorce, but if the marriage endures, it will be better than ever.

EQUALITY AND RESPECT

I keep finding my thoughts returning to one of today's most prominent women, Hillary Clinton. Hillary and sexism go hand in hand. Is she a presidential candidate or a "female presidential candidate?" Could she have been a presidential candidate if she hadn't put up with her husband's shenanigans or double standards? Women have to be shrewd and divisive, but then they are thought of badly. Sitting quietly in the background has not worked. Being abrasive may not be the best choice, but right now it is the *only* choice to make way for generations of younger women so they can be in the middle—not abrasive, not confrontational. But first we have to unplug the resistance. We both have to fight generational obstacles—me with age, Hillary with gender.

What's the choice? To make changes, like getting a divorce, or to be oppressed. Today's women have careers and relationship equality. But that was not the case for Hillary or for me; we both had to struggle against the message of the time, which was to stay home and take care of it. That's what my therapist said I was supposed to do, but that statement didn't help me or my relationship with a controlling husband. If the therapist had been a woman, would he have said the same thing?

Equality in the home exists only if you get respect, and respect is directly related to high-powered careers or a status that is considered high. Hillary's ambition was her career, and her marriage was part of that ambition. Mine was marriage, family, and career. It has been a hardship, juggling them.

CHECKLISTS

Consider these two lists, which I think nicely summarize the best traits and the worst ones that a woman can find in a husband. These lists, developed by Millard J. Bienvenu, Sr., are directly linked to the idea of respect.

The most happily married woman says she has a husband who:

- Discusses how family income should be spent.

- Discusses his work and interest with her.
- Helps with cooking chores and shares mealtime, with easy and pleasant conversation.
- Understands her feelings.
- Listens to what she has to say.
- Pays her compliments and says nice things to her.
- Is affectionate toward her.
- Waits for her to finish talking before he responds.
- Allows her to pursue her own interests and activities even if they are different than his.
- Lifts her spirits when she is depressed or discouraged.
- Allows her to let him know when she is pleased with him.
- Disagrees with her without losing his temper — and makes sure it works the other way, too.
- Discusses problems without losing control of his emotions.
- Offers her cooperation, encouragement, and emotional support in her role as a wife.
- Can tell what kind of day she has had without asking.
- Engages in outside interests and activities with her.
- Lets her know that she is important to him.
- Knows what she is trying to say.
- Talks about things that are interesting to both of them.
- Discusses sexual matters together.
- Discusses personal problems.
- Admits it when he knows he is wrong about something.
- Sits down just to talk things over.
- Spends several hours together with quality time, doing what they both enjoy.

The least happily married woman has a partner who:

- Makes her keep her feelings to herself.
- Uses a tone that is irritating to her.
- Is difficult and makes her keep after him about his faults.
- Doesn't discuss feeling and attitudes.
- Remains silent for long periods when they are angry with one another.
- Makes her avoid expressing disagreement with him because she is afraid he will get angry.
- Complains that she doesn't understand him.
- Argues a lot over money.
- Makes it difficult to express her feelings.
- Insults her when she gets angry.
- Makes it easier to confide in a friend than in him.
- Confides in others rather than in her.
- Monopolizes the conversation.
- Sulks and pouts a lot.
- Doesn't let her discuss certain things because he is afraid that she may hurt his feelings.

Does your husband listen to you? Making decisions with money and planning for the family are all qualities that describe successful marriages. Does your husband try to control you? Keep you away from your friends? Tell you what to say, what to wear? Don't feel complimented that he cares. He is trying to possess you, and when he doesn't like what he sees, you'll have a high price to pay.

Taking turns being supportive, nurturing, and nurtured is the only way a marriage works. These are the right role models for children. A child often represents the environment of home, and that environment can be changed.

The need for respect goes both ways. Not only do men need to respect their wives, but vice versa. If respect is not shown in a marriage, and this lack of respect is deep-rooted and pervasive, then—as I tell my clients—it may be time to consider moving on. As times change, and we no longer have to stay in marriages out of economic necessity, respectful partnerships are an absolute must. Getting older gives us the perspective to understand this, and to take action to empower ourselves.

10

Find New Words for Old Age

As I compiled research and explored my own thoughts on marriage and happiness, I couldn't help noticing how age played a major role in this area. Women are constantly pigeonholed by their age, or at least perceive that they are. (And these insights confirm my belief that having children later in life can be the right move for some.)

As middle age gets extended and old age shortens, and as more and more reproductive options come to light, there will likely be many more "grannymoms" in years to come. The message we project shapes the message we get back. Age is in the mind. Feeling young can happen at any age. Not only can we live longer, but we can live healthier, too. What we do with those extra years is up to us.

Among the older women I counsel, even the word "grandmother" feels wrong. They want to be called "baba" or something else, as they imagine a "grandmother" is someone who sits at home in a rocking chair, knitting. They are hungry for a vocabulary that describes them as what they are: vital, strong people who are capable of starting new things. Rightly, they feel that now is *their* peak time; they have the whole package. They are feeling passion that they never had before, are experiencing depth of feeling they never thought possible, and are making big changes. The word "grandmother," on the other hand, makes them feel disempowered.

Many of these women are in a better place than ever before because their family and childcare responsibilities have lessened. Often, I see that when couples age together, relationships are reversed: the woman feels more empowered, as the man takes a step or two back.

My clients are seeking a new vocabulary to describe their stage in life largely because they want to express a changing reality: after forty, fifty, sixty, and seventy, one does not have to decline. In fact, what used to be thought of as old age is now arguably our peak years.

PEAK YEARS

When I was a bride and then a young mother, I was supposed to be happy to be linked to such an ambitious man. But something bothered me about that, even though I didn't quite know what it was.

Now, I know what that look on my face was all about. I wanted to have my own identity. I couldn't stomach the idea of being dependent on my husband; intrinsically, it just felt very wrong. But society told me otherwise. I had to be militant or be a homemaker. That was the only choice. But I listened to my own inner voice, and I did both, but with much struggle. As a young mom, I remember how critically other mothers would in my apartment building would look at me, knowing that I was going to school while they were wheeling their toddlers around town all day. What might be considered common today, my ambitious nature, was uncommon then. No one asked why my husband was not helping out; responsibility for the children was mine alone, or so I thought.

I had to face a major conflict between my inner voice and society's voice. I have always had to struggle to make changes before they were accepted. I listened to myself and became a mother and a career person, struggling with pressure from all sides and from myself. Now that I have a family and a career, society is telling me I'm too old to be ambitious again—this time when it comes to motherhood. Sorry, but I did not plan on getting old at sixty.

"Grannymom" is obviously offensive, "grandmother" less obviously but understandably so . . . but what about the word "middle-aged"? Even that word troubles some of my clients. The term implies that we are headed for a slump, and that the only way is down, when in fact the opposite is true: if you are in so-called middle age, then chances are you are peaking.

Your productivity, wisdom, and looks are finally your own. You know your style. But the beauty of it all is that you are still growing. Taking that knowledge without looking for approval from anyone but yourself is wonderful. No one can tell you what is good for you except you.

"Move over," the younger generation can seem to be saying, "It's my turn." But the older generation is saying the same thing. Each has a lot to offer. The only difference is that when you're older, you have a perspective that you didn't have before.

It used to be that when you were of a certain age, you had expected to be taking care of your children's lives, their children, and their celebrations. I will never forget one day when my sister was over with her grown children. She kept saying proudly, "Now it's *their* turn."

This is a common refrain. But I was turned off by her message. After all the years of motherhood and sacrifice, I thought, it was now *her* turn. I finally know myself and I am supposed to give that up? No, I told myself. It will be both their turn *and* my turn, and no one will suffer.

For me, having the twins was symbolic of women determined to live their lives not younger but better. My emotional, financial, and physical resources have peaked, so isn't this the best time to use them? When you're at your best and can contribute the most, society gives women a different message. After all, heads of corporations, presidents, and leaders are all in their peak years. That's when we have the whole package.

11

At Home,
Let Happiness Happen

No one can make you less than you are, unless you allow that to happen. Consider the following case study:

Ever since she was a child, Beverly was contradicted. Because of this, she never trusted her judgment. If she decided to eat lunch out with her husband and chose a French restaurant and he, in turn chose an Italian place to eat, she made the wrong decision and she should have chosen an Italian restaurant. Beverly often pondered over her indecisiveness and this drove her husband, Jack, crazy. After a while, he had trouble taking his wife seriously and made most of the decisions.

You need to make your own decisions to make things happen rather than allow things to happen to you. It is always harder to live by someone else's mistakes.

Scott is very abusive. He constantly ridicules Jean, telling her what to do. He does not let her see friends unless he feels it is the right time or if he likes them. He does not let her talk on the phone with her parents if the conversation goes too long. He does not give her enough money to buy clothes for the children, etc. One of Scott's methods of keeping Jean under his control is to tell her not to talk with anyone. If people know they have marriage problems, friends will think less of her. What he is not telling her is that he wants to keep the problems to himself so other people won't find out how evil he really is.

If you try to keep peace, you will become the rescuer. Why should he try so hard when you do all the work?

Susan always makes certain that her husband's responsibilities become hers. This way she won't have to be disappointed. When it's time to take care of the children, she makes certain she is in charge. Yet she complains. He will never take over if he doesn't have to. Susan needs to take the chance of having things not work out perfectly. As long as she needs to have things done by her own standards, she will be disappointed. She needs to trust her husband and take the chance that his way is different than hers, not any less perfect.

Keep your marriage low-maintenance. Don't look into his eyes so much, thus allowing yourself to be "sucked in."

Vicky was always concerned about what her husband was thinking. Was he happy? What could she do to make him feel better? Because of her feelings, Tim, her husband, would always be demanding. He knew Vicky was always there for him. After a while, Vicky was so affected by her husband's needs that whenever they had a disagreement, she could not tolerate his resentfulness. Vicky felt that if her husband was happy, she would be too. She gave all her power away.

Women often fail to see their situation, but lack the strength to do anything about it. Why do women perceive their situation as they do, and how do they decide among conflicting interests they confront? Some women are passively coerced while others conform actively to traditional social arrangements. Others contribute to social change by refusing to acquiesce.

Men who work often feel they are doing what needs to be accomplished. Women often feel they still are not in control of the decisions, where the money is going, and how much needs to be spent. They still have the problems of child-caring and household responsibilities. Men often do not have to deal with issues outside the workplace.

Although Emma worked, she never asked her husband to help her with the children or household tasks, feeling that if she complained too much, she could lose her husband. Without him, she would never have the same financial security. He paid her for almost everything and therefore felt he deserved respect.

When a woman works, does she feel her job is accommodating her needs, or does she feel that the pressures continue in spite of the work she puts in? If she does not feel her job is securing her needs, the feeling of hopeless-ness will prevail in other areas as well.

Women who are mothers produce daughters with mothering capacities and the desire to "mother." By con-trast, though, those women produce sons whose nurturing capacities and needs have been curtailed and suppressed. This prepares men for their less effective family role and for the participation in the impersonal world of work and public life. The modern woman experiences inner and outer pulls as she strives towards individuation.

What is labeled as masculine behavior is generally highly regarded and rewarded in our society. The girl who excels in school or is athletic, receives approval. There-fore, the "feminine" role is not consistently reinforced. If wider social values conflict with feminine attributes, ambivalence is a likely outcome.

When Nelly is at work, she is in constant conflict with herself in that she feels she should be home with the chil-dren. When she is home, she wonders whether she is reach-ing her potential at work. Nelly is confused about her role and where she should be. What Nelly doesn't realize is that as long as she takes care of both at different times, no one will lose out.

As you plan for the future, reach goals together. Take turns supporting each other's goals. Remember, whom-ever is more successful has the obligation to bring the other person along. Feeling free of guilt or prejudices no matter what road in life you take will make you happier, just as long as the changes each person makes allow the opportunity for the other person to be part of them.

Nancy became an investment banker before marriage and she returned to her field after her children entered school. She finds that her responsibilities involve traveling, so instead of having to choose between a family and a career, whenever possible Nancy takes her husband and children along. This way, even when her husband or family cannot come along, they feel they have an understanding of what Nancy is doing and an option to be part of it next time.

In order to overcome these blockages, a woman must know what she wants. She should ask herself: How much time do you want to devote to work, to your family? Then find a position that allows you to have the schedule you need. Realize that you may have to work around your career or family, but children do get older and grow up. Also, it is important to know what it is you need from your husband. Do you want him to come home earlier? Do you need him to change his days at work or to change his job? As women have more equally paying jobs, their decisions at home should be more equal. Remember both of your careers are important, so he may have to do some changing at his job as well.

Paula, a successful doctor, has already raised her family. The kids are well adjusted, her marriage is intact, and she is enjoying her life more than ever. One important ingredient that Paula possesses is that her husband, John, is very supportive of her. He helps with the chores and children, making life much easier.

If the husband wants more children, if he likes his wife working, then this is usually what happens. If you are supported in what you do, then the struggle is cut in half!

Listen to where your partner is coming from. You don't have to agree; just try to understand and be willing to work with him. Don't take everything personally. Complaints are often a way of crying out to be heard. Remember, it is the silent ones that throw you the surprises. Even if he is complaining, at least you have something to work on.

Karen was constantly worried that Troy would say something negative about her, and she refused to take him into consideration when he spoke to her. She just wanted to make sure Troy would understand her. What she was missing at this time was a chance to make the marriage better.

Don't compete. There is no right or wrong way of doing things. The differences each of you have to offer the other will help you bring different insights into each other's world.

Moreen always felt intimidated when her husband disagreed with her, almost as if he were saying she was stupid. She had trouble doing anything he wanted that was different than what she wanted. She felt he was keeping score. Moreen missed out on letting herself learn from another person's perspective.

The marriage is heightened when each person learns to appreciate his or her own uniqueness. Each person can appreciate and respect each other's individuality. This knowledge affirms their differences and promotes receptivity to the other and creates intimacy.

Diane used to be resentful when her husband would get up in the morning to go to work. She would watch him leave the house, all dressed up with his briefcase in hand.

She was jealous that he would be able to have time out for lunch and that he could develop a different side to himself. What she didn't know was that he also worked very hard and also envied her being at home. They each wanted a part of what the other had.

There is a fine line between becoming independent or dependent. Suffocating each other or being too neglectful of each other are ways to destroy a relationship. Self-definition, a general freedom from ascribed roles, the capacity to understand and sympathize with the aspirations of women, were the attributes husbands held that most enabled women to work outside the home.

Sharon's husband, Ken, was a teacher. Ken was used to seeing women at work. He saw them as equal to him. Ken admired these women and was also proud of Sharon's accomplishments and independence.

A married woman's career level is positively associated with her education and negatively associated with the number of children she has. Dependency, detachment, and expansiveness ought to be understood. All three are healthy needs that one must acquire for happiness. Detachment is the desire to be alone and a need for self-sufficiency. Expansiveness involves growth, self-assertion, mastery, and expression of appropriate aggression, all necessary in the development of a healthy personality. The decision to choose any one over the other tends to create a neurotic character pattern.

Men traditionally take on the detached role and women are often the dependent personality. This can result in conflicts. Freud reinforced the concept in women's dependency needs by claiming those needs are biologically based. Healthy dependency is the ability to express feeling, the need to be close, to be loved, and to love.

You do not have to be a clone of your partner. On the contrary, it will add more color, more luster, to your relationship if you present ideas and experiences that the other person does not possess. Think of it as a gift, as something different that the other person may never receive otherwise.

When I was a young mother, I wondered why I needed to go beyond my family to fulfill myself while other mothers seemed more content. I found out that women who have more prior conflict from their mother's unhappiness working in the home were more motivated to work outside the home and had to use a masculine part of themselves to do so. Those who were taught to have a career from the beginning had more androgynous traits, while those whose mothers were contented working in the home had more feminine qualities and were also happier working in the home.

Janet was always motivated, wanting to be an attorney. She went to law school after marriage and when her children were old enough to attend school. Her husband, who was also an attorney, felt threatened and worried that he might lose her. The prospect of change was almost going to cause a divorce, but as her husband became less threatened, he saw that he had a happier life. This motivated him to spend more time with her and the children. As Janet became more independent, her husband became more nurturing. They were each happier as they each fulfilled other parts of themselves.

Love enriches our lives, giving us happiness. In the neurotic, the need for love is increased. A neurotic is dependent on love. He overvalues love. Love includes giving spontaneously of oneself to people, a cause, or an idea. The neurotic is not able to do this.

Women overvalue love. They want everything from one partner. They want love and security, yet they yearn for independence, thus setting themselves up for disappointment. The key to women's growth is to let go of the demands on others and to find security in themselves. Then love will follow. Power dependency or withdrawal from people would not be a problem if we had enough love in our earlier years.

Samantha had lunch with her friends about once a week, but when all else was said, the topic would be focused on whether they were happy or disappointed with their husbands. I am certain that if their husbands got together, their wives might have been a point of their discussion—but not the focus of their discussion.

These women would often identify themselves with how their husbands treated them. Instead of being part of the relationship and part of their lives, their husbands became everything in their lives. Samantha would vent about what her husband did not do, or what he needs to do for her, without ever realizing that anything he did should not have been expected but appreciated. The only expectation she could have was from her own self.

12

Defy Double Standards

ALTHOUGH THINGS HAVE CHANGED TREMENDOUSLY since my mother's time, and even since I became a mother in my late twenties, in my view, gender-based double standards still exist. They are just harder to see. The challenge for us as we get older is to challenge the double standards which we may have been brought up to consider normal. (You know how I feel about "normal.")

For instance, when it comes to housework, women have often had to take on the lion's share while men simply come home at the end of their workday. Did the careers that we strove for give us equality, or are there still double standards today? You would think the housework would be equally shared, but practice lags behind theory sometimes.

When it comes to housework and childcare, we cannot ignore the fact that double standards still exist. Women who work outside the home still do more household chores than their husbands because they feel a need to prove themselves as good wives and mothers. The higher the career status the more likely women are to get outside help and the more likely women are to have control over decisions, vacations, and money. They will be heard and listened to in a way that housewives often are not.

HOLLYWOOD RELATIONSHIPS

Time was when "May-December" relationships almost always meant an older man paired with a younger woman. But that's slowly changing to include older women paired with younger men.

Usually, it starts in Hollywood and is then filtered down to more common folk. Consider the following list of famous older woman–younger man couples. Even the ones who have split garnered some important attention, contravening the traditional double standard:

Twelve years apart:
Daryl Hannah and David Blaine
Susan Sarandon and Tim Robbins
Dorothy Squires and Roger Moore

Fourteen years apart:
Rosanne Barr and Ben Thomas

Chrissie Hynde and Lucho Brieva
Bernadette Peters and Michael Wittenberg
Mira Sorvino and Chris Backus
Raquel Welch and Richard Palme

Fifteen years apart:
Brigitte Nielsen and Mattia Dessi

Sixteen years apart:
Ruth Gordon and Garson Kanin
Tina Turner and Erwin Bach
Heidi Van Pelt and Taran Noah Smith

Seventeen years apart:
Katie Couric and Brooks Perlin
Isadora Duncan and Sergei Esenin
Vanna White and Colby Donaldson

Eighteen years apart:
Francesca Annis and Ralph Fiennes
Juliet Mills and Maxwell Caulfield
Mary Tylor Moore and S. Robert Levine
Norma Shearer and Martin Arrounge
Dinah Shore and Burt Reynolds
Elizabeth Taylor and Larry Fortensk

Twenty years apart:
Lorraine Bracco and Jaeson Cipolla
Edith Piaf and Theo Sarapo

. . . And the list of past and present Hollywood couples who dodged the double standard goes on.

It has been hard not to feel frustrated when people have criticized me for having kids at sixty more than they would criticize a man. Once, for instance, I was on the radio explaining why I'd had kids after sixty. On the air with me was Rod Stewart, whose seventh child was born when he was sixty, his eighth at sixty-six. But no one mentioned it. Older men had always fathered babies later in life, and have been celebrated for it. In the future, I wonder whether older women could have babies later and be celebrated as well.

Sexual desirability is also being redefined; traditionally, I always thought a man could have a paunch and still feel sexual, but a woman with a bulging waist was looked at as matronly.

The list of double standards seems to go on and on. A man who climbs the ladder of success and has a family is considered a family man, but a woman who does the same thing is often seen as selfish. And in my mother's time, women who made more money than their husbands were often shunned by other women—and by men as well. These women were often in less of a rush to marry; they don't need to trade their independence for economic gains.

THE SHADOW OF SEXISM

Society has difficulty in dealing with the uniqueness of women, the new and the different. Until very recently, sexist attitudes dominated our society. The world has far to go; these things do not change overnight.

Until recently women were not hired at top-level positions because men felt their menstrual cycle would get in their way of making the right decisions. The old religious conviction of women walking behind men while out in public and covering their entire body is still being practiced today. It's almost a sin in at least two countries to have a female baby; often, the children are killed or the mothers are forced to abort.

What's more, women are often seen as frauds. One good friend of mine who is also a psychoanalyst, constantly has to explain her background to others. People question where she went to school, how she got where she is, and how long it took her to get there. The feeling is that if she could do it, anyone could do it. Oddly enough, her husband, who is psychoanalyst too, has never in his whole career been asked any one of those questions.

Another indication that sexism is alive and well: according to my clients, ambitious women are often thought to use manipulation and sexual charm to gain what they want, but are suspicious of fellow women who they consider to be similarly manipulative. It is a vicious cycle which perpetuates the idea that professionally successful women are calculating and fraudulent.

Through my research I found that those women who were most competitive did not have careers and were often the least secure. Women's social, political and economic status will help them to become increasingly satisfied with themselves and more secure.

The list of double standards and sexist stereotypes goes on. If a man is good looking, he is not considered less intelligent and is often promoted for his personality and impression. A good-looking woman would often be taken less seriously:

Debbie was a very attractive 49-year-old, with long, straight blonde hair. She carried herself with confidence and was soft-spoken. Whenever she made a personal call to market her herbal vitamins, she did not fare as well as her male friend who represented the same product. Debbie chose to dress more conservatively by pinning her hair back, applying less makeup, and wearing clothes hiding her body. To her disappointment, sales started getting better! Although she is doing very well in sales, Debbie must continue wearing drab clothing and keeping her looks in the background.

Face facts: until a mere fifteen or twenty years ago, a woman often got her needs met only by getting a man to take care of her. Today she has the education, training and experience necessary to be a highly productive career person. Many of us who have not chosen this route, assume those that did only got there through manipulation. After all, how could we women playing at career people actually have 'the right stuff'? According to the traditional pattern, the husband is older, more educated, more intelligent and successful than his wife and thus maintains a superior status.

Most girls grow up suppressing themselves and their development to placate and appease their parents and the men to whom they have become attached. Most women are not aware of the price they have paid until they attempt to change. The process of change stirs up anxiety and reveals depression. The growth a woman is attempting to foster can endanger the only identity with which she could be comfortable. Rejection because of gender is not the only reason for the high incidence of depression among women, but it is intensified by the experience of growing up in a culture of prejudice.

With awareness and change, double standards can keep fading away. Women are now leaving husbands or lovers more so than ever before. They are finding men they spend more time with at work far more interesting and exciting.

When men pursued a career, the entire family was oriented toward helping him. And often when a woman would begin her career, it was not uncommon to drop out of medical school when getting married or drop out of practice for eight to ten years to take care of her family.

A woman with masculine characteristics has much higher assertive traits and more of a need to go out and develop a sense of herself than a woman with feminine qualities.

Girls are often brought up to be both career-oriented and caretakers, while boys are brought up to be focused solely on careers. That is why, among my patients, divorce often leads each person to try and fill the missing part of themselves. Newly divorced men often look to have a relationship.

Women, on the other hand, follow a different pattern after divorce: they usually look to fulfill themselves, to have a new career, to attend school, to nurture their individuality. Often this is because their characters and careers have been put on the back burner, despite their very best efforts and despite the pervasive illusion that things have changed.

What's more, when a man needs to move because of work, the whole family moves. When a woman needs to relocate for work, that is often not as easy.

Today women are looking for a man to be equal in nurturing, attractiveness, and productivity. But when we deny that double standards still exist, we limit the progress we can make. We are still at the crossroads of change, and as we get older many of us realize that we need to actively dodge the double standards around us; they will not dissipate completely just because times are changing.

Sadly, what I see in my psychotherapy practice today is not so different from what I learned from those questionnaires I sent out so many years ago. Unfairly enough, women who earn more money than men are still sometimes seen as a threat to other men as well as to women.

Despite the push for equality, I think that women look at love differently. To women, love becomes everything they are. To men, it is just one part of who they are. Women often become dependent, while men start out that way and remain dependent. But dependency can become a problem. You want the other person to be everything for you, but controlling that person is the only way you know how to do it. That is why men distance themselves and women become pursuers. It's best to be both—dependent and independent, each person taking turns to nurture and support the other.

In *Jonathan Livingston Seagull*, Richard Back wrote that a bird that flies away from the flock is considered independent, but if it were a female it would be considered deviant. Susan B. Anthony said of her father, "If I were a man, he would have been proud of me. But as a woman, I am looked at as defying womanhood." She led the way towards the women's movement.

HILLARY CLINTON

Hillary Clinton is subjected to double standards. As a strong woman she is often derided as aggressive, while a man would be considered assertive; selfish though a man would be considered selfless; not a good mother while a man would be considered a family man.

In my opinion, Hillary dared to look away from her relationship in order to achieve her goals. I could not. I wanted both a good relationship and a high-powered career. The relationship got in my way, and it took a lot of work. But nothing has gotten in Hillary's way, and I commend her for that. She could have worked on her marriage, even left her husband after his infidelity, but her energy would have been taken away from her political aspirations. She had no time for that. She had to make a bigger difference to the world. She has been strongly criticized for this by other women.

Sadly, a woman often has to make a choice. Bill Clinton was caught up in the old boys' network. But, unlike in earlier times, people no longer looked away. Hillary had to look away in order to keep energy directed at her campaign. I tried to do both and suffered the consequences of trusting my husband to make the right decisions for me. (That didn't work. "If you get famous, I may have to leave you," he once said. So trusting him like I did, I spent my energy on the family.)

I compromised my career to have a family and a relationship. Hillary compromised her relationship to have a career. We both missed out. Today, women have both family and high-status careers without compromise. As we get older, it is important to make sure that we are no longer falling prey to gender-based double standards, which can manifest themselves in obvious as well as subtle ways. Instead, demand equality.

I was brought up in a generation with double standards. I tried to break away. I fought for career and family, for equality in a relationship and a high-status career. I definitely did not get approval, many years ago, when I was pushing for it; I faced the stigma that working while having children was not acceptable. Having an equal relationship was not the proper role model, and making more money than your husband was not widely accepted. I have always tried to embrace change, even when it scared me to make changes.

Now, in considering questions of ageism in the years since giving birth at sixty, I feel like the stigma against older women starting new things is comparable to the stigma I felt against ambitious women back in my twenties, when I wanted to be more than "just a housewife." I hope that will also change.

13

Cultivate Character
(And a Career)

IN MY RESEARCH AND PRACTICE—AND RIGHT IN MY
very own family—I found that women are excessively
focused on others. As a result, their needs are often
repressed. They seek the approval of others so they will
not be rejected, and this serves to keep their dependency
needs intact. Women are constantly worrying about
what other people think of them, and this detracts from
their inner sense of self.

We have traditionally limited our use of independent
thought because of fear of rejection and being alone.

And traditionally, we felt the need to be taken care
of, but success on the job may give us a different message. If a woman's main ambitions are to find a man

so as not to have to be independent, she will face major conflict.

There are ways that we perpetuate dependency from generation to generation. A mother, for instance, may be envious that her daughter has opportunities she didn't have. I remember, for instance, how my mother vetoed my trying out for plays, going on a cruise to ballroom dance, and so much more, saying that she had not had these same opportunities. In response, a young girl may want to please her mother and try to stay dependent. Today we enter roles that require assertiveness and aggression, skills that have always been recognized as necessary tools for *males* to succeed.

Traditionally, I've seen that men derive self-esteem from love. A woman, by possessing an ever-diminishing faith in the worth of her abilities, can never be happy in love alone.

A marriage is heightened when each person learns to appreciate his or her own uniqueness. This knowledge affirms the differences of the two people, makes each more receptive to the other, and creates intimacy. As a person's needs are fulfilled, interest in others will grow.

Stacy is a physician, achieving prominence in her career after marriage. Stacy's husband, who is in a less prestigious field, stepped back to give her career top priority. In time, there was an apparent reversal of roles, and she began to refer to him as househusband. Soon, a lack of respect developed for him, which manifested itself in reccurring extramarital affairs. More recently, Stacy has felt that she already had sown her wild oats and is interested in returning to her marital relationship. This is what is happening more often, since women have taken on prestigious work.

Often we marry for love and security, yet we yearn for independence. We want everything from our partner, but our partner cannot possibly have everything we need. We want our partner to make up for our past, our unresolved experiences. Anxiety is the connection for this increased need for love.

We distrust our partners because we expect too much. This draws our energy and we feel helpless to meet life. We shift our responsibility to the man. Such a woman dominates her husband, and he may eventually hate her for this. The man may fall into a trap of his own, expecting giving and devotion but deeply resenting the dependency.

Rosanne was dependent on her husband for everything. She had difficulty making any decision without him. When she found out her husband had an affair, she was shocked. The other woman was much older and not half as good-looking as she was. Rosanne later found out that her husband was too overwhelmed with her needs and enjoyed being with someone who had something to contribute intellectually.

Only future role models of equality for both sexes will alleviate much pain in these kinds of relationships. The man must also know how to take care of, support, and nurture the relationship, and the woman must also know how to carry the responsibilities.

"WHO AM I?"

These are only words to the dependent person who stares with amazement when such alternatives are offered.

Dependent people are severely alienated from their inner resources; their sense of emptiness is so painful that they cannot comprehend what these possibilities are referring to.

This also explains their terror on being alone. To be alone is to experience an unbearable void. Since they do not experience their identity, except in terms of others, they feel at their best when taking care of a husband or child. They focus almost exclusively on externals and others. They can be easily convinced that plastic surgery, new clothes or other people will solve their problems, making them feel better. They throw all their energies into finding a mate, then into changing him, shaping their children and, if possible, changing the attitudes of everyone around them. They guard against inner and outer change as rigidly as they can.

The more dependent the individual, the more controlling he or she becomes. Some become phobic or merely live a marginal existence with an undercurrent of severe anxiety and depression. They live in a fear of spontaneity. They fear unfamiliar impulses will carry them out of control or lead them into acts that are disapproved of by others. This further restricts them, making it difficult to handle new experiences.

No one is perfect, though many may demand perfection from a spouse. *We must learn to let go of demands of others and, unless we do, there will be little happiness in a marriage.* If you do not love and understand yourself, no one will love or understand you.

Our culture has not made it comfortable for a woman to seek her own individuality. Freud stated that men have more polygamous dispositions. Was this a self-fulfilling prophecy? When society gives a message, that message becomes appropriate behavior. Women were not given the same message. It is not a coincidence that families having a history of unfaithful men have fostered children with the same history. Eventually, this even becomes genetic. In reality, women have more physical potential to be polygamous. I have contact with couples in my office and find that women are the ones who are predominately having affairs. It is not the passivity of women that has kept them behind, but men's desires often demand that women be passive and weak.

Today, society is giving a different message. Men who have sexual escapades while married do so because they are sexually addicted and need treatment. Unlike the era when Jack Kennedy had double standards, Bill Clinton proved that our society has changed and this behavior is no longer acceptable.

Katheryn often stayed late to complete her work. When she came home, she was excited about her day, while her husband, Dan, was ready to sleep. She had no one to converse with, and her loneliness increased. Katheryn realized that she did not want to leave the marriage, but she was also aware that she was attracted to a very handsome man, Bob, at work.

At first Katheryn started having lunch with this male. She needed desperately to have someone to talk with, someone who would be interested in what she had to say. Bob fulfilled that role, listening to what she had to say. This made Katheryn feel closer to Bob. She was able to get from him what she could not get from her husband. Bob gave her support, love, and recognition. They soon became lovers. Katheryn never left her husband because she also loved him, but in a different way. Her emotional and sexual needs were finally met.

It is time to view yourself in a different way. You can be both feminine and assertive in a positive way. During the feminist movement, women gave up the pursuit of marriage by having careers. Today, a new generation of young women is choosing to stay part-time or full-time at home and raise their children, keeping the marriage intact. What will happen to these young women when they reach their thirties or forties? My practice is filled with such women who ask, "What happened to me along the way? Somehow I got lost in the shuffle."

Pat was a well-trained real estate woman, who put her career aside to raise her children. She came to me and felt that her life was over and that she had not done enough with it. Her children were off to college. What was left for Pat now? She had not established a close relationship with her husband. The family was everything. She became over-weight, absorbed herself in her children's lives, and did not like or respect who she had become.

Although Pat felt it was too late, she soon discovered that she could bring back the old Pat, the Pat who liked to meet new inner challenges through a new career or hobby. She did not have to stay where she was—stuck in life. As I saw her through the years, she started looking and feeling younger, acting more spirited.

The late thirties is often a time of crisis in a marriage. Often, the children have outgrown their need to be cared for in the same way they needed caring from you before. You are forced to face yourself, your husband, and your lifestyle. There are no more distractions. The future you were building together when you were younger is here. This person you are now left with is the one you have to face every day. Do you really like what you see? It is a time to build new beginnings and new visions for the future together. Many people have difficulty doing this. Women often get a divorce in order to do this. They don't know if they can make these changes with the man they are with. They need help.

Rosa is in her late forties. Her husband, Bill, is successful. She sees herself as a good person and doesn't want to appear selfish. She was taught to take care of others and told me that she enjoys taking care of others. Bill and their daughter, Adriana, who are both outgoing and happy with themselves, see her as a problem person. She is often complaining or unhappy.

Rosa's son, Anthony, is much like her. He presently has changed several jobs and had been staying with Adriana while attending school to study physical therapy. When he called off his engagement with a girl his sister liked, his sister stopped talking to him, and he moved back in with his mother and father.

Rosa and her husband were immigrants from Europe. She questions her need to stand up for herself. After all, her parents had to endure harder times in the old country, so who was she to complain? However, she is in pain about the way her son is treated by both her husband and daughter.

During her child-caring years, Rosa lived next door to her mother-in-law. Adriana would often go next door instead of coming home from school, especially when the aroma of her grandmother's cooking wafted through the neighborhood.

Rosa's pleas to her husband were not heard. He did not want to disappoint his mother by telling her of Rosa's request that her granddaughter, Adriana, no longer was permitted to visit her after school. Adriana, her father, and his mother soon became a triangle. Rosa was powerless. She hated her mother-in-law and felt pushed around by her husband. She also felt her daughter was too opinionated about her mother's and father's life. When she told her daughter to do something, including coming straight home from school, she was expected to obey but didn't.

Anthony had also become a problem child, someone who had no regard for his mother's orders. Rosa needed a way to regain her power. Her husband needed to support Rosa regarding Adriana and Anthony. Both children needed to see a solid relationship between their mother and father to regain respect for her mother. As Rosa became stronger, she was able to put herself first without feeling selfish. She was to become a loving matriarch. Adriana and Anthony began to soften a little. Both did not have to identify with their father's strengths but began to see a side of their mother they liked, the strength and sensitivity for her family.

As Rosa continues to change, so will the dynamics within the family. It is like a domino effect. When one domino changes position, the others fall behind and into place.

Assertiveness does not mean being negative. It means being a person, accountable for being responsible and, in return, being accepted.

Reeva was seeing a married man. He said he promised to divorce his wife. Reeva was willing to stay with him forever. He came over a couple of nights a week, and she paid for all the food and other expenses. He was a dentist and said he could not afford to pay for anything. Reeva was a massage therapist, having little money herself. Even when he told her she had to wait until he could afford to marry her and leave his wife, she believed him.

When Reeva finally told Bill she was going to date other people unless he gave her a commitment, he refused, and she realized that Bill was never going to leave his wife. After some therapy, Reeva met Marty, a pleasant man who, unlike all the other men she knew, was not controlling and was concerned about her feelings. His interest in health and nutrition went well with her approach to massage therapy. They opened a health clinic together for yoga and massage therapy. Reeva is beginning to find trust with a man once more. After living with Marty for one year, Reeva is beginning to see that a monogamous relationship does not have to be either boring or destructive.

Betsy was married for twenty years and has five children. She was also able to work as a nurse. Her husband worked hard making a good living, but Betsy never felt he was taking care of her. He bought himself a boat, even though she argued that they needed that money for household expenses. Her husband is generous with the children, but when it comes to his wife, he is very withholding.

Through an investment, Betsy now has some money of her own. Because of this, every time she needs money for something extra, he tells her to take it from her own account.

Betsy is bitter, and this has prevented her from enjoying her husband's company. She does not trust him. Betsy has come to realize that if her husband felt she really needed the money, he would be there for her and his intentions are not to work against her. Rather than remain bitter and hold back from enjoyment of her own life, she has accepted that this is who she is married to and is taking better care of herself by purchasing the frivolous items she previously was afraid to buy. All the time, she knew that if she really needed her husband, he would be there for her.

Women are not the only ones to look back with regret. Men do, too. Roy is an example:

Roy was overweight, overworked, and over-dedicated to his wife. Every day, he would commute for one hour to the city, often with just enough money in his pocket to get home. While at work, he took abuse from his boss. He had difficulty sleeping because he feared losing his job and having no resource to support his family.

His wife, Jennifer, was self-absorbed, exercised every day, worked for a dentist, and put her own money into clothes and luxuries for herself, purchasing a fur coat and diamond bracelet. Jennifer described Roy as being fat, short, gray, and ugly.

Today, Roy works locally and spends his lunch hours going home—to walk the dogs, to work out, or to work on himself in therapy. He has turned all his fat into muscle. His hair has been dyed to a light brown, and he looks like *a younger version of what he was. He now buys himself clothes, jewelry, and other items he desires. He never goes around without at least $100 in his pocket. He even takes vacations once a year, without his wife. His new confidence has brought Roy success at work as well, and he has gotten raises through the years. His wife now contributes finan-cially to the family, and she believes that her husband "is the greatest."*

Relationships are not always easy, and they are so closely linked with our day-to-day happiness. When it comes to improving them and cultivating harmony in the home (and, with it, inner peace), it helps to understand the complex dynamics that exist between men and women. As we get older, we have the chance to understand these dynamics more and more deeply. Wisdom, born not just from research but also from hard-won experience, is one of the many advantages of growing older.

CARE ABOUT YOUR CAREER

As a research psychologist, I've always been interested in equality for women. I investigated women and happi-ness—how women could have it all in careers and family, how we strove for equality and got it. But did we? Every angle I looked at kept leading to age discrimination. Women are still being treated differently when it comes to age. We are just starting to make headway by having high-status careers and, therefore, more power in society. But has anything really changed for the ordinary house-wife and her status? When it comes to age, men are still treated differently. Women are getting older when they have babies and are leading productive lives in the work-place longer.

My life didn't unfold the way I came to wish it had; I wish I had developed a career earlier. I always protected my parents, then other people. I found myself doing what others wanted and expected, and what I wanted always got in my way. Remember how my mother-in-law had quipped "as long as you're having fun" when I embarked on that PhD? My career was not dealt with as an important thing, only as a fun diversion, by my in-laws and my husband. Nor was my career. Today, though, women are young and vital, no matter what their age. They can celebrate—and can be celebrated—in their lives. It is no longer everyone else's turn; it's my turn. No questions asked, no approval needed. As women make more money they will have more power in their lives.

The happiest women I found were the ones who had both a career and a family. And you need to develop a sense of yourself before you can develop a career and a family.

My research has shown that the most depressed men are those who must retire and that the most depressed women are those with less than a high school education who have preschool children at home. But the happiest marriages are those where the husband and wife take turns supporting each other and nurturing each other. Children also thrive when the parent of the opposite sex supports and encourages them. Being productive and channeling your energy are what life is all about; other-wise, our minds atrophy, just as the muscles in your body atrophy without exercise.

Women now come to me asking what happened along the way. They ask: Where am I going? My children are grown, but where am I?

Throughout my life, I've always had inclinations of wanting to contribute—to my parents, my family, and to the world at large. I have always felt I have not done enough, that I needed to do more.

BREAK THE OLD RULES ABOUT MARRIAGE AND CAREER

My own upbringing gave me the impression that most women, including my mother and older sisters, followed the rules that were laid out for them. They were mothers and homemakers, and occasionally they took jobs to supplement the family income. Ordinary women, such as my mother and her family, did not aspire to play a part in what was then the new women's movement. They did not become professional career women.

Times have changed. When I graduated high school, I was told to get my "Mrs." But by the time my daughter graduated, she was expected to have a career first, then a relationship and a family.

Women, I have found, are still struggling to understand their roles in light of this change. Some of this has to do with society, some with a woman's background. Many women who had traditional mothers who stayed home with the children even if they were frustrated about this had to recreate the dynamics with males, sometimes forcing themselves to act aggressive, overtly intelligent, or competitive, in order to pursue professional careers. In my research and through seeing clients, I saw how this *could be* devastating to a marriage as the woman assumes more self-identity and power. This may be a casualty of contemporary families trying to adjust to changing times, without attending closely to how this impacts their dynamics in subtle ways.

I have found that a man marries a woman with the hope that she will not change but that a woman marries a man in order to change him. What usually happens in a marriage, though, is that the woman changes and the man stays the same. So what happens when the woman wants to change? Men marry women for certain specific reasons of their own. For example, some want to have dinner on the table each night, with the children and wife waiting for him. And when the original reasons clash with the reality, problems often begin.

I changed. I had babies later on. And when I took advantage of all the media opportunities that followed, it ended up having positive ripple effects on just my self-confidence, but my marriage too.

This is not unique. It is consistent with the research I had carried out for *What Price Power*, my study on the changing nature of women, career, and home life. In case you need some persuasion that pursuing an edifying career has myriad positive effects, I offer the following evidence—in addition, of course, to the case study of my own life. New advances in reproductive technology, which let women break free from biological clock concerns, go hand in hand with these findings.

CAREER WOMEN WIN AT HOME

Most of the attention paid to feminism since the 1960s focused on the workplace. When I did my research on women and happiness, I discovered that women who had more power *outside* the home had more power *inside* it, too. As women are getting more prestigious positions in the workplace, there are lifestyle shifts as well. Instead, they are able to make decisions based on themselves, their families, and their spouses. I wrote about these lifestyle changes and my findings in my book *What Price Power*, and a lot of these choices for women still apply today.

The findings of my studies revealed profound change in relationships when women went from being extreme housewives to focused professionals. I also discovered that women who fulfilled themselves after marriage in less extreme circumstances, meaning any woman who raised her status in the professional world, also changed her relationships for the better. At home, women with careers were valued more, their financial and social decisions carried more weight, and the marriage genuinely felt more equitable. Husbands, in these situations, shared more in household tasks and in childcare.

Eighty-one percent of my survey respondents, all professional women, indicated that their mothers who worked seemed to enjoy working. 43.5 percent of the female professional workers reported that they were the oldest children in their families, compared to 23.2% reporting that they were the youngest.

Among these same respondents, entering a profession had not interfered with having children, as only 12.9% of married professional females in my study reported that they had no children. In fact, 30.7% reported having three or more children, consistent with the typical suburban family size; 40.7% reported having two children; and 15% said they had one child. 78 percent said that they had satisfactory communication with their husbands.

My research found that professional women had better marital relationships in terms of communication, defined by the ability to exchange meaning and feeling with their husbands as well as having equal say in financial and social decisions. It showed that the happiest women were those that had both a career and a relationship and a family (and that age had nothing to do with it). So for any woman out there who is still putting anxiety about starting a family ahead of her own professional ambitions, my advice is: don't do it. There are, after all, other options.

14

"Confess" Your Age

WHEN I FIRST HAD THE TWINS AND GOT CAUGHT up in a publicity firestorm, my age terrified people. People really freaked out about it, and at first their reaction made me feel incredibly insecure. After all, I had learned to lie about my age for so many years.

I had always been given the message that getting older meant disintegrating. It definitely didn't mean starting life again. Getting older was negative, bad for you, maybe even fatal. At sixty—let's face it, even at only fifty—many of us are told that we are has-beens, and that we should just move to the background and be quiet.

Admittedly, when people openly mocked me for daring to give birth at sixty and refusing to apologize for it, I thought, "Really?" It was frustrating. I did not want to be labeled as "old," and certainly not called the "granny-mom." I had wanted to be seen as beautiful, sexy, smart, educated and talented—but I was sixty. I had strived for those things all of my life, and now that I was feeling confident, why did my age have to be a stigma? I did not feel confident in these qualities when I was young, and at sixty, when I felt more confident than ever, people picked on my age?!

When the media attention started, my life changed drastically. The book I had written about equality in marriage, *What Price Power*, was being translated for readers around the world. I went on speaking tours. Television and radio stations called to ask my opinion on things, and I was even asked to consider a movie or TV series. I would watch the news in the morning to catch up on current events in preparation for being called as a commentator. My ambitiousness and curiosity about the world had been reignited. My husband was proud, my adult children were impressed, my young children saw me engaged and happy. But best of all, I was feeling more vital than ever.

Eventually, something clicked. When people called me the "grannymom," I said to myself: *To hell with that*.

I hope it does not sound vain to say it, but: I even feel that I *look* better as I get older. My clothes fit me differently. They just look better on me. I am in love with life, with myself and everyone else around me. I find myself blowing kisses instead of saying goodbye. I have finally arrived. The true me has come out of the closet. I wonder if other people have this kind of response in their lives.

My experiences have led to a list of my ten tips for redefining life after sixty, or at any age—at least for redefining mine.

1. Age has nothing to do with anything.
2. Make changes every five years.
3. Get healthy emotionally, so that you can have an emotionally healthy relationship.
4. Look at your own individual stage rather than your age in order to make the right decisions.
5. If you are feeling "old," remember that each new decade brings a new stage that is different and unknown. Embrace the newness, and you will not fall into a pattern that does not represent you. When you look back, you will see how young you really were. The problem is that a person a decade older than you seems old, or does until you get there yourself.
6. Don't let others tell you who or where you should be in life.
7. No one has the answers except you.
8. Speak softly and with confidence; people who are loud or hysterical are not heard.
9. Reach goals.
10. Act on your feelings if you want a relationship, a family, or to be productive in other ways.

To change your life at absolutely any age, don't just complain; do something about it. Most importantly, never stop trying new things or making changes. At least, that's what I tell my daughter.

DON'T BE AFRAID

I often hid my age, or even lied about it. I always feared that revealing my age would categorize me as being something I was not. Society dictates the stage of life where you're supposed to be and the age you're supposed to have attained when you get there. But what happens when that does not apply? What about late bloomers? I am a psychoanalyst, not a psychologist. I deal with the individual, not with some template that dictates what someone is supposed to do at a certain stage of life. What works for one person does not work for everyone.

I put my husband through law school—put up with difficult in-laws, protected and defended my parents, whom I saw as physically and religiously vulnerable, took care of my children, put myself through a PhD program. Does that mean I can never listen to myself? Who are all these people, telling me what to do? By being myself I will be making it easier for future generations in my family to avoid imprisoning themselves.

Early on, I did not plan on having babies at sixty, but what if I did something else that was not expected? Who should be my boss? The answer: me. I do not need anyone's permission to do something. And I don't want to hear anyone tell me that it is their turn now. It is everyone's turn, all the time. I will be damned if anyone else tries to tell me what is best for me.

What really impressed me were the women who called to say that I gave them the message to go ahead and enjoy their lives and be who they want to be. They feel young and vital, but they felt they needed permission from society. But society has few role models for women getting older. Not only are there just a few, but those few are extremely well known. The trick, of course, is to follow their example, even in the absence of their fame.

When you're thirty, you feel that it's your turn to make changes. But that doesn't mean that someone who is thirty should deny those same choices to someone who's sixty. In fact, when these thirty-year-olds turn sixty, they will probably look back and say that they had no idea just how young you really were. I wish I had just relaxed about my age and enjoyed where I was. Women often live in such fear of getting older that they deny themselves the pleasure of enjoying where they are in life.

Age is being redefined. When I was quoted in *Newsweek* after giving birth to the twins, I realized not only that there is life after sixty but that life may just be *beginning* at sixty. You can make new choices. You can go back to school, start a new career, move to a new town, get a divorce, fall in love, reinvent yourself . . . anything is possible.

I often find that my clients' own inner voices—the intuition they may have squelched for so any years— already have the answers. Often we look to other people, like authority figures, to give us permission to move forward. But an "authority" is no longer necessary to tell you who you are. When you reach a certain age, *you* are the authority. This knowledge will free you, so instead of being afraid of getting older, you can embrace the upcoming years with anticipation of better things ahead, just like a person in her twenties or thirties would do naturally.

The sad thing is that even younger people fear aging. They live with that fear for the rest of their lives, and as they get older that deep dread gets worse and worse. But it doesn't have to be that way. We can reinvent ourselves and discover a new view on happiness and vitality at any age.

As I got older, I feared becoming "invisible." I'm not alone; a lot of women harbor this same worry.

But now I regret having worried so long about feeling invisible at a certain age. Because the fact remains: we are only invisible if we let ourselves become that way. If we look "frumpy" and act that way, then that will dictate how we will be treated. If we respect ourselves, others will respect us.

Many of us have been taught to *give* throughout our lives—to put the needs of others before our own. Even though I wanted so badly to distinguish myself and cultivate a career before I got married, I was always told "no" and pressured to look a certain way, act a certain way, and not ask questions or complain. Even when I was in my twenties and dressed to the nines, sometimes—because I was not expressing myself of speaking up—I felt invisible. Even in my wedding dress that everyone praised as being so beautiful, I felt a little lost and confused.

As I got older and learned to prioritize my own happiness, a funny thing happened: everyone around me seemed to be paying more attention. More and more, I felt *seen*.

So why are those who look better less invisible? After all, you have to be more self-involved in order to take care of yourself. As women, we are often taught that it is selfish to take care of ourselves. We are taught to be selfless, or else no one will like us. So, again, society gives a double message: *No one will like you if you are self-centered. But we respect a woman who takes care of herself.* That double message is confusing.

Having pride in yourself is not selfish. Giving all of yourself to others does not get respect. It is best, I have found, to be in the middle. There is a fine line between neglecting yourself and taking care of *only* yourself. The old saying that the more you give, the more you get doesn't work. Not only does it not work, but it can often work against you. Respect for others comes from respecting yourself first.

What people say and what they mean are often two different things. The harsh reality, at least as far as I see it, is that some men *say* they want their wives at home with the children, but then they respect the woman who is dressed beautifully and is productive outside the home.

It brings to mind a patient who sent his wife roses when she was rehearsing for a play. He treated her like gold, sending her in a limousine to arrive at a party with some famous guests. But when she stopped acting to please him and worked at home with the children, his celebration of her was over. One day while they were on vacation, as she was doing a children-related errand, he stated, "You can help. You have nothing to do anyway." She felt invisible in that moment.

When a woman gets married, she often wants to change the man; when a man gets married, he wants his wife to stay the same. But what often happens is that he stays the same, she changes, and problems begin.

Sometimes, the way to seem more visible is to go back to the time when you were younger. How much time did you spend on yourself? Did you buy yourself new seasonal clothing? Did you make sure your weight was where you wanted it? Was it important to you? Yes, your life may be busier now. You can be a wonderful mother, wife, career person, daughter, and more, but that doesn't mean you can't appreciate both the outer and inner beauty in yourself. You don't have to make a choice.

Women as a group have been taught to neglect themselves for the sake of others. Women often come to me and ask what happened to them along the way. They bemoan having gotten lost in the shuffle. Only if you keep working on yourself can you prevent this. Go to school. Take on a job or career. Be willing to change your goals and reinvent yourself every five years. That will keep you from feeling "invisible."

Take chances and make changes in your style and your pursuits, and your inner glow will come through. If you feel lackluster, others will also see you that way. What you project is what you get back. (Or you can always move to Europe, where older women are more respected, seen as sexual, and date younger men!) There is no reason not to see older people as attractive, vibrant, and fulfilling.

Just because you are told that something is over doesn't mean that it is. All too often, women who are mothers have absorbed the message that they should disappear after their mothering was done. Getting older without fulfilling ourselves is something that we need to address. Today, women have other extensions of themselves on which to focus. To feel more *seen,* it is vital to establish a place for yourself while your children are in school. Go back to school; seek something that you identify with for the future. The empty nest does not have to mean an empty person. And as many of my clients found out first-hand, taking good care of oneself is the ultimate turn-on.

REDEFINING SEXINESS

Today, older women have so many options. My older clients' options are no different from those of younger women; it's just that they don't know it. If life and health are extended, why shouldn't a woman extend her own lifestyle? The only person limiting that is you. If you wait for permission, you may never get it. Society has always found it hard to accept changes, and women have been less assertive in letting those changes happen.

Older women have a mystique about them. A friend of mine said he saw Sophia Loren at the airport. The way she walked and carried herself showed that she was seasoned in knowing who she was. Older women often have a confidence that is sexy. They no longer have the need to fit in. They know who they are and what they want. Lots of women can look great when they are young, but looking great when you are older represents who you really are. It is something that identifies you individually; you are your own person. You no longer have to follow the trends. You know who you are. Your goals, orientations, accomplishments—these are what define you. Age is just a passage of time. It is not an extension of who you are. It is just a number that no longer explains who we are today.

Today, more women than ever are getting married later, having families later. Their prime years are later. The new fertility treatments are creating equality for women by letting them postpone the baby-bearing years. Women have often been judged by their fertility. Now, with new technology, this is changing. Fertility, productivity, and aggression used to be exclusive to men as they got older. This no longer applies. Women have caught up. The boundaries between getting older and being vital have been blurred.

Attractiveness is based on fertility and sexuality. As women are able to reproduce into later years, just as men do, the double standards will start to shift. Men can no longer hold the rein for reproduction. Younger women no longer need to be the only solution for older fatherhood.

Freud said you have to work first in order to play. You have to feel a sense of productivity and then you can enjoy yourself. Men are most depressed when they are no longer productive. Being a sexual human being is vital to feeling productive. Sexuality comes with assertiveness and power. Women as a whole are gaining their power by increasing their longevity with fertility, sexuality, and productivity.

Those of us who have observed what it means to be a wife and mother over generations have seen things swing around on a pendulum. First it was marriage, family. Then it was marriage, career, family. Now it is career, relationship, family. By the time women are getting around to marriage, they feel their time is scarce for finding the right man. My research found that the happiest women valued both career and family.

What is sexy? Sexy means having confidence, control, independence, and experience. Those qualities improve as the years go by.

15

Get Pissed Off

GLORIA STEINEM FAMOUSLY SAID THAT THE TRUTH will set you free but first you have to get pissed off. Well, I am pissed off that all these years I was defined by my age. I bought into the myth I should represent myself as being as young as possible.

I'm pissed off that many of us spend our lives fearing getting older and then look back with regret to see that we were not that old. I'm pissed off that women are still defined by their age instead of their intellect. I'm more pissed off that many women buy into that.

I never listened to what society told me, anyway. I went back to school when there was a stigma for women to work and have a family. I later researched and found that children of working mothers were using them as role models and that made them stronger. I wanted equality and a high-status career, but I never listened or waited for society to tell me it was okay. Now, career and family are the norm, but if I had waited, I might have missed out. We are still lagging on what I'll call age equality. No one asked my husband how old he was when I had twins at sixty, even though he was "old" too at sixty-three. Women are still being treated differently if they reveal their age. Many women don't; they keep it a secret for fear of facing discrimination.

THE S WORD

When I had Josh and Jaret, online commenters couldn't stop calling me the S word. I guess I shouldn't have been all that shocked by the disapproval people expressed. But I was thunderstruck that the average person called me extremely *selfish*.

I remember when I was in a Manhattan café, and a man asked me whether I'd heard about the old lady who had twins at sixty. "She must be crazy," he said. "Who is going to take care of them when she gets older and when she dies? Will the government have to foot the bill? Who helped her to become pregnant, anyway? They should have his license taken away. The fertility clinic should be closed down. They should take the kids away from her. What about all these poor babies in orphanages? How selfish. She could have adopted an older child. That would have been more responsible and more age-appropriate." When I told him I was that crazy old mom, he could not stop apologizing.

I imagined all the other conversations that were happening in other cafes. People speculated that I had the babies to get attention, make a movie, or earn a lot of money. I responded to all those accusations. But they kept coming.

People kept speculating about why I did it. Most speculation was wrong. It wasn't to make a revolutionary statement, to show it was possible, or to be a medical outlier. I did it neither to be defiant, nor to prove anything. Not because I greedily wanted to have as many kids as possible. Not because I was absolutely sure at the time that I could handle it (though things had gone well with Ari, I wasn't totally sure about anything). I didn't do it to look younger, or to get a reality show or my own movie, as some suggested. It wasn't because I had so much love to give that I wanted to give more, or about my ego, or that I wanted to be loved unconditionally. . . .

I did it largely because my husband and I both wanted it so badly. Together, we were determined.

I grew up during a time when men treated women unequally. But within our marriage, Ken and I endeavored to assign equal value to our respective desires. Fortunately, we shared a common desire to add to our family. At sixty, I wanted to adopt, while he thought I should try to give birth again. (It always felt strange when people who read about my giving birth to the twins at sixty, or watched news stories about it, called me "selfish"; in fact, my husband was the driving force behind the birth. It's possible he wanted them even more than I did.)

I was told I was selfish when I went back to school, selfish when I had a career, selfish when I wanted equality in my relationship and selfish when I had twins at sixty. But if I were to retire in Florida away from my children, stop working and having fun, would that not be selfish? If I were to build my life based on other people's opinions, I would be endlessly confused.

Florida? On some days, Florida sounds pretty good. *Just give me a life of fun and relaxation,* I think when I'm busy with public speaking, television shows, driving kids around, cooking, listening to complaints, falling over at the end of the day and then starting over again at the crack of dawn. Sometimes I would rather be free, on vacation, having my meals served to me. I would have fun and possibly be the *youngest* in the group. Maybe then I wouldn't be seen as selfish?

As I mentioned, a great deal of this decision was driven by Ari's needs; I wanted him to have a sibling. I made a decision that many women would not make. As a result, I am *not* on a vacation (or, sadly, in Florida). I'm working hard to make these kids happy and to have enough energy to get their needs met. Putting someone in a pigeonhole and locking them in—to me, *that's* selfish. On bad days, I wished I could ask some of the more vicious online commenters: *Does saying I'm selfish make you more comfortable where you are in your life? Just because you don't want to take a risk doesn't mean that someone else shouldn't, does it?*

The world said I was old, selfish, and crazy because I had babies at sixty. So what? We are living longer, but we are healthier than our parents were at the same age. There was a time when women lived only to about forty. So, yes, they were "old" if they had their children after age twenty. After chopping the wood, feeding the chickens, milking the cows, sewing, making dinner, and doing the laundry and the dishes, they were exhausted. Childbirth was often fatal. But times have changed.

And in my opinion, they have changed for the better. To my children—from Jaeson all the way down to Jaret and Josh—it might seem like a given that both men and women have their own hopes and dreams, their own educational endeavors and career goals; for women, there is more to life than being a wife and mother. The capacity that women have to make a difference in the world in myriad ways is—in our culture, at least—embraced without controversy. But the messages that I received when I was young, just one generation ago, sometimes seemed to be telling a different story. And for my mother, I imagine that options for self-determination felt narrower still. It's important to stop and think about how quickly the tide has turned, and how it continues to turn.

Almost lost in all the attention that came my way for giving birth at age sixty is how radical it was for me to have given birth at fifty-three. Now, it's not so revolutionary, but it sure was at the time. The age "sixty" struck a nerve. Many women who responded negatively to my giving birth at that age acted like I was taking away something that belonged to them, as if motherhood were a zero sum game.

I am not an expert on fertility techniques, but I do know that they can be expensive and therefore not available to all women. I hope that as time goes on, options like freezing eggs, using donor eggs, and undergoing in vitro fertilization will become more widely available and affordable. I am not saying everyone should have babies later in life. But I am an advocate for increasing the options that are available to women.

16

Revolutionary Motherhood?

NINE YEARS HAVE PASSED SINCE I RAISED EYEBROWS around the world by having twins at sixty years old. Now, at sixty-nine years old, I take stock.

I have five children, and got famous for having two of them late in life. But, like every other woman reading this, I am also so much more than a mother. I have a longstanding career as a psychotherapist, with people coming to my home office with all sorts of problems and leaving with different perspectives on those problems. I have a PhD in psychology, plus lots of research on women and happiness. I took a risk when I became a mother at fifty-three. Seven years later I did it again, and went through a bizarre period of being scrutinized by media all over the world. With my husband of more than forty years I went through many different stages.

Since turning sixty, I have not hidden myself away. And I have been careful not to keep my feelings inside, like so many women before me have done. In fact, I have cultivated a career in the media as "Dr. Frieda," appearing on radio and television shows across the United States where I weigh in on all kinds of current events.

I participate in a public speaking group (and won an award), enjoy giving talks at my synagogue, and have gotten involved in local politics to the point where I was asked to run for town council. Recently I served on a committee to help choose and elect my town's mayor.

Since turning sixty, I feel increasingly *inspired*. I am very involved with the twins' homework, teachers, playdates, and weekend activities, seeing psychotherapy clients in my home office while they are at school. We take them bowling, golfing, sledding, and on all kinds of adventures.

Sometimes, during a rare quiet moment, I think about that woman in front of me on line at the supermarket, whom I saw when I was in my early thirties. I remember how euphoric she seemed, and how unsettled that had made me feel. I'll also remember the woman in my building's elevator who turned her nose up at my leaving young children with a sitter as I rushed off to school. Back then, I didn't understand *why* these experiences unsettled me. But I do understand that, at sixty-nine, they wouldn't bother me today.

"You just want to be a housewife," my husband had said all those years ago. He may have been teasing, but this struck a nerve. As happy as I may have been, I also felt trapped. And I set out to prove him wrong. I did both, going for the college degree I wanted but also having time with the children. I also waited for them to start school before I trained as a psychotherapist. I wanted to keep learning, constantly searching for what would bring happiness—not just to me, but to everyone else who was searching.

Back then, I was tuned in to what other people thought of me, perhaps hypercritical to any judgments about me "as a woman," whatever that means. Back then, I suppose, being a woman meant being a perfect housewife, infinitely attentive to her children and taking care of all the cooking, cleaning, and nurturing while her husband paid the bills.

Now, I know that molds were meant to be broken and no one is perfect. I am proud that I pursued all those years of schooling and then embarked on a career—while I had Jaeson and Alana. I am glad that my psychotherapeutic career was up and running when I gave birth to Ari at fifty-three through IVF. And, despite what the many, *many* skeptical commenters thought, my famous (infamous?) multiple birth at sixty made life better than ever for my whole family.

When I was still in the delivery room, before the C-section had even been finished, the press was already making statements about me (fortunately, they declared the babies to be "beautiful"). I was asked to conduct a press conference. They all wanted to know how I did it. A woman from another part of the hospital wrote to me. A woman from Pennsylvania wanted to come to the bris. A nurse stayed up and talked to me the whole night. I was sleepy, but she was enthusiastic.

The hospital had to hire a special switchboard operator just for me, and the morning after I gave birth, *Today* and *Good Morning, America* were there by five, with other major shows soon following. It was so chaotic that a bodyguard was installed the hospital door. Inside the hospital, I was transported through a little-known tunnel, but the press was waiting for me at home.

They were so hungry to interview me — but remember: it wasn't because they wanted to wish me well. Rather, most of their questions implied that I had done something wrong. They wanted to know why I had chosen this path, whether I believed I would live long enough to adequately care for the twins, whether I was being selfish, and what my other, older children thought. But putting myself out there was worth the risk; I knew that by sharing my story, I could make a difference. There was a chance, however small, that what I said in those interviews could inspire and empower people, or maybe just one person — regardless of what they had to say about my age.

I know that it won't be long before it's no longer considered revolutionary to have a baby when you're older than fifty. Even in the decade after Ari was born, it had become far less astounding. Having a baby even at age forty was pretty revolutionary during my mother's time.

I am part of a very small population starting this new path for motherhood. But my generation of women has always been on the cutting edge of change. We were the

first to have real careers, demand equality in our relationships, and demand equal pay. We could be feminine and
assertive at the same time. Now, we are making newer
changes through the years. We are redefining ageism and
making a path for others to follow, in my view, and that
makes me feel good.

As time goes on, I won't be so unusual. I predict that
in the coming years we will see a rise in older mothers.
Some will be single and others who will have partners.
Some will have already established themselves in careers,
having made no compromises for family life, while others
will be entirely focused on being at home . . . entirely by
choice.

The rise in older motherhood reflects a new way of
looking at life, ambition, and relationships. Starting something new is possible at absolutely any age.

PART III

SIXTY THINGS I LEARNED
AFTER SIXTY

"Age," Reborn

"Know that you are the perfect age. Each year is special and precious for you shall only live it once. Be comfortable with growing older."
— Louise Hay, bestselling author

When I gave birth to Josh and Jaret at sixty years old, many people scratched their heads about whether I would be able to keep up with them. But amid the chaos of changing diapers *again* and running after kids *again* (and this time a pair of them), something pretty amazing happened. I surprised myself and rose to the challenge, and then some. And if I can do that, anyone can.

At sixty-nine, I feel I have more potential than ever, and am more excited than ever about my life. I credit all this to tuning into the lessons I learned *after* I turned sixty. (Yes, it took me a while to understand some things, and I am still learning to the point where I may need to make a similar list at seventy.)

The great part about getting older is that we learn to trust our own judgment, something that society tells many of us — especially women — *not* to do. Whatever your age, chances are you can easily make your own long list, too.

1 Not too long ago, forty was considered "old." Back in 1932, the psychologist Walter B. Pitkin published a book called *Life Begins at Forty*. It was a number one best-seller that year. Although he did not invent the phrase "life begins at forty," his book put it into the popular lexicon. It became a catchphrase, with its influence felt well into the twenty-first century. According to Wikipedia, his book title was lent to "a 1935 Will Rogers movie, a 1937 song sung by Sophie Tucker, a 1980 John Lennon song, two television series (in 1978 in Britain and 2003 in Hong Kong), and several novels and other books."

The book made waves and had a ripple effect, in my view, because it gave voice to the idea that attitude was everything. During the year of the book's publication, average life expectancy at birth in the United States was only sixty years of age. Lifestyles were harder, casualties were greater, and (of course) the medical world was less advanced. The idea that life could remain fulfilling after the age of forty was a revolutionary one. Can you believe that was less than a hundred years ago? Where will be in another hundred years?

Even though the book needs to be updated today, the sense of empowerment that *Life Begins at Forty* gave people was not baseless, in my opinion. There is no reason to feel that life is over at a certain age. And times have changed so much since that book was published.

2 Average longevity is rising fast. People under the age of, say, thirty-five may think that sixty is over the hill. But for those of us in our seventh decade, it does not feel that way. Sixty-four percent of people over sixty-five say that they are enjoying life more than they did just after turning fifty. Older people are happier, more confident, and more adventurous than ever before. A time of life that would once have been seen as "twilight" is now viewed as a time of adventure, opportunity and change. The average longevity of our population is rising fast: by six hours every day.

3 . . . Really fast. Two-thirds of all men and women who have lived beyond the age of sixty-five in the entire history of the world are alive today. This includes forty-five thousand Americans over the age of one hundred. One million baby boomers will reach the century mark.

4 Happiness may be U-shaped over our lifespans. In the *Daily Mirror Online*, I once read about a British study showing that self-reported happiness is U-shaped over the course of our lives. The study said that happiness is at its highest during youth and older age and that it bottoms out during the middle of our lives. Enjoyment of life began to rise around age fifty and was still rising up to age eighty-five. While I am not sure what kind of metric measured happiness in this study, the results seem plausible. With so many advances in health care, we no longer have to spend our older years held back by ailments, or worrying that they will crush us when and if they strike.

5 Levels of stress and anger go down after people reach their early twenties, according to the article. This chimes with my personal experience: for so many of us, the extent to which we worry—sweating the small stuff, basically—declines steeply after the age of fifty. As levels of stress worry and anger drop, levels of happiness and enjoyment increase in our fifties and sixties.

6 We grow more adventurous over time. I've read other studies indicating that increased life expectancy and early retirement have created a much greater emphasis on quality of life. Despite years passing, people increasingly feel vibrant and are adopting pleasure-seeking attitudes; that *Daily Mirror* article said that eighty percent of people over the age of fifty report being "more adventurous" about life as they get older. This may be attributable to having more free time to have fun, to the joy of becoming grandparents (or in my case, a plain old parent too), and to having more financial stability. Ninety-two percent of women in their fifties reported being happier than ever before, and four in five feel just as sexy as they felt in their twenties.

7 And we become more assertive and confident with age. I've seen that in my friends and in my clients, and I've felt it very strongly in myself. Good news!

8 Attitude can really inform how old or young we feel. In my opinion, Walter B. Pitkin's influential book was right on that count, even though today it is obvious to all of us that forty-year-olds are far from finished enjoying life. For me, becoming a mother again at sixty, and all the other things I did since that big birthday, have proved that we should not accept any kind of limitation placed on us because of our age.

Pregnancy and Parenting

Because I've had the rare (and, in my mother's words, "crazy") experience of experiencing pregnancy in my twenties, thirties, fifties, *and* sixties, people sometimes ask me how this experience has changed over time. Each time, it has been hard and also wonderful. Looking back, there are some things I wish I'd known the first time around.

9 My last pregnancy brought the same food cravings I'd had during previous pregnancies. Each time it was the same: I wanted chicken thighs, and frozen grapes or grape bars.

10 Discomfort can become manageable. When pregnant with the twins, I got nauseous in the first trimester, but didn't take medication because this time I knew it would pass. When I was pregnant with Jaeson back in my twenties, I found the nausea hard to handle. My doctor prescribed a pill. I am happy I didn't take it, since I later read that that particular medication could lead to deformities. But I believe that women should do what is right for them, and there is nothing wrong with asking for help.

11 Babies' scary health problems can turn out just fine. One of my twins was colicky early on. I would walk the hall with him all night, exhausted. I gave him juice instead of milk as the doctor suggested. He ended up with rotten teeth. When the doctors wanted to do surgery and take them all out, I declined, and fortunately the new grown-in ones look great. The first time around, I was incredibly nervous that something would go wrong with my babies' health, and might have decided to go ahead with the operation out of fear. But with the twins things were less nerve-racking, and I was able to let myself wait and see.

12 There are more middle-aged moms around. At school drop-off and pick-up, at PTA and volunteering events, and pretty much everywhere else, I see many mothers past their forties. In fact, I rarely see mothers who look to be in their twenties.

13 "Normal" pregnancy is becoming abnormal. The process of having a child has changed so much since I first gave birth. In vitro fertilization like I went through with Ari, Josh, and Jaret is on the rise, but other experiences like adoption or surrogacy are more visible, too. Tyra Banks, for instance, just famously had a son through surrogacy. In having twins at sixty, I may be an outlier, but I am not unique. More and more, I hear about older parents, same-sex parents, and parents with wide age gaps between them having kids.

14 These days, men are "pregnant," too. When had my first child, fathers or partners were not allowed in the delivery room. Now husbands say, "*We* are having a baby." This is a good thing.

My mother took care of all the cooking, cleaning and child care in our household. Today, by contrast, women are not expected to be sole caretakers of their young children. Men do not want to miss out, and increasingly they do not feel it is okay to shove that work (joyful as it can be at times) onto their wives. For more and more men, including my husband, parenting is something in which to take pride.

15 Dads are in school. In contrast to my experience with my older children, the classmates of Josh and Jaret have dads who get involved with events, homework help, and parent meetings.

16 Pregnancy is on display. When I was pregnant while younger, I hid my pregnancy as if in shame. For some reason, I just felt really embarrassed about that big bump, like it made me less pretty or something. So I wore loose tops. But today, the image of pregnancy has become somewhat more glamorous. Women wear stretch tops to show off their bumps, and I love it.

17 We parent with more purpose now. When Jaeson and Alana were young, the concept of the "play date" was not so widespread, nor was it take as seriously as it is today. In the suburbs of New Jersey where we live, I notice that among the parents of Josh and Jaret it is almost as children's activities are more important than those of the parents. Sometimes I think parents need to relax; play dates can be fun, but they do not need to be serious business.

Parents and tutors do homework with their children at an alarming rate. As a result, when it comes to the kids' performance in school, the children are often given credit for the work of their parents, or in the case of many kids in my area, their tutors. (I am not a fan of too much homework; I believe that after school, kids should be able to go off and play or do whatever they want to do, without every moment being "scheduled" for productivity.)

18 Children are savvy, not sheltered. At nine years old, Josh and Jaret know things I did not know at their age and still do not know. Information is instantly available at their fingertips; they seem to be constantly checking things out on the internet. So as much as we want to shelter and protect them from certain things, sometimes they find out on their own.

19 Households seem increasingly to be centered around children, whereas in my parents' time they were more centered around the grown-ups' schedules. No more sending the kids to bed after dinner so the parents can talk quietly over drinks.

20 The unexpected will happen. I had eight nannies the first few years. Each one left under a different odd circumstance.

One came with a bible in her hand and soon after was walking around in baby-doll pajamas and had an affair with the gardener. Another, who was so overweight that she broke the chair she was sitting in, decided to leave because of a health problem. Yet another snuck food in the room and then disappeared one day without notice. Another nanny would routinely take large stretches of time to visit her family in Poland. Nanny number five sang loudly and badly while she vacuumed and one day I heard her singing while she was filling up my tub so she could take a bath, even though she had her own room and bathtub, which rubbed me the wrong way. Another one drank our vodka and kept filling the bottles with water. Another one left crying, complaining that she had washed hundreds of loads of laundry. Yet another nanny left most of the work for me to do, and when one evening I found myself running after the children while she leisurely ate dinner with my husband, it was not a great feeling; she then left for the neighbor and took my expensive watch. Eventually I decided to stick to babysitters.

21 Sibling relationships are not always perfect. Disagreeing with my decision to become a mother at sixty, my oldest son Jaeson did not want anything to do with the twins at first. Despite living close by with his wife Michelle, he stayed away from Josh or Jaret for the first three years of their lives. During family holidays, the twins stayed upstairs; in fact, they were so scared to be seen by my son and his wife that they would zoom up the steps to their room every time they came over. Wanting to keep my oldest son and his family happy, I played a role in keeping the twins away from them and would urge them to play upstairs. That makes me feel incredibly guilty.

One day, Jaeson was in our kitchen and bumped into Josh and Jaret by mistake. They started to run upstairs as usual, but Jaeson asked them to stay. He chatted with them for a while and realized that he could not hold a grudge.

Now, they get along well. But the road to get there was rocky, and sometimes I wonder and worry about what was going through the twins' heads when they were sent upstairs. With members of my family at odds, it was impossible at the time to make everyone happy at once.

22 Kids don't always make sense. The twins look very different and have different personalities. When meeting them for the first time, many people are surprised that they are even brothers. Jaret has brown hair, brown eyes, and an olive complexion, while Josh has blue eyes, light hair, and fair skin. One looks like me, the other like my husband. They also introduced my grandchildren as their nieces until I told them to just say "cousins." Sometimes, imitating my son Jaeson's children, they call me "bubby," but then say they don't like hearing me called that. I just have to laugh.

Marriage, and How It Evolves

Many of my psychotherapy clients are working through issues with their marriages, which I guess is not that surprising as I live in the suburbs. My own marriage, which has lasted more than forty years and which has had many different stages and twists and turns, has taught me a lot, too. When I wrote a book on marriage, *What Price Power*, I got to explore the results of those surveys I sent out a long time ago with the help of a statistician. The experience of researching and writing that book gave me an illuminating look at the changing dynamics between men and women. The book concluded that women who focus on their careers are happier at home too, and I still believe that. But since turning sixty, I've been thinking about some other aspects of marriage, too.

23 Marriage is endlessly complicated. Many couples come from vastly different upbringings and have experienced the world in completely different ways, yet expect to have similar views on issues of childcare and much more. This is unrealistic; things are so much more complicated than they first appear. I feel that couples should see a therapist before they get married, to learn how to communicate and compromise. Every marriage involves many moving parts, but with some work and careful scrutiny you can often figure out how to make those parts work together.

24 My husband's qualities make up for what I don't have. It took me a while to realize just how much Ken's personality traits differ from mine; maybe, looking back, we chose each other because of the complementarity of our traits. For instance, he is very detail-oriented, while I am very spontaneous. Lots of times our differences have gotten on my nerves. Couples should learn from each other's differences, rather than competing. I am still learning this lesson well into my sixties.

25 Divorce is less messy these days. Growing up, I thought of divorce as a tragic problem akin to having a serious disease. My parents taught me to stay in a marriage because it was sacred. People used to stay in hard or unhappy relationships because divorce was so messy, but now that it's more widespread, I hope that my clients (and anyone in any unhappy relationship) know that there are solutions. Divorce can still be mess, and sometimes it results from arguments over trivial issues. But it can be rewarding for some.

26 Focus on the future. Many of my clients marry people just like their mothers or fathers, and then try to fix what they were not able to fix in their families or origin. This is a common mistake: we should focus on our future, not our pasts.

27 There's no "right" or "wrong" time to have kids. Couples often ask if it is the "right time" to have children. I used to think there was a "right time," but since turning sixty I've realized that there is no single "right time" — nor is there a "wrong time;" I'm living proof of that.

28 We should not expect perfection. Once, at an Orthodox Jewish wedding, one of the other guests made a casual comment that stuck with me. "Marrying someone is like buying shoes," she said. "If you see a pair you like, buy it. Chances are you will have to keep looking and wear your feet off if you do find anything as nice. The chances of getting what you see is far better and more convenient." Although I generally believe in the adage "Don't marry because it is the right time, marry because it is the right one," I wonder if the truth lies somewhere in between these two perspectives. In the happiest marriages, at any rate, I've noticed that both partners subscribe to a sort of eighty percent rule: they expect a good effort from their partners, but they don't expect perfection. We don't need to sweat the small stuff.

Instead of expecting perfection, I try to just be honest, trust, and don't expect too much. That's my current prescription for long-term love, at least.

29 Avoid boringness like the plague. I used to think that it might be boring to be married; in contrast, single life appeared much more exciting. But marriage is far from boring; in fact, it is often a roller coaster and you are in for a ride. One of my clients had feared marriage because she dreaded a life of "boredom." But once she took the plunge, life seemed *more* exciting: the couple went into the health business together, went on long hikes, and shared new adventures. In my case, the more exciting (and chaotic) my life gets, the more I have to talk to my husband about at the end of the day. All of the television and radio work I take on, for instance, has been good for us.

Marriage is more exciting when both partners are individually fulfilled. In my parents' generation, women were taught to give, while men were taught to self-fulfill. From my first pregnancy to becoming a mother again at sixty, I have seen this norm shift in significant ways just by watching the people around me. This shift is, in my view, very healthy. Mothers have a right to seek fulfillment in many different arenas, not just when it comes to their kids.

30 Embracing idiosyncrasy is romantic. My father used to give my mother an unusual Valentines's Day card. He would take her to the drug store, she would read it and he would put it back. They both felt better knowing he did not have to pay for it. Instead of a box of Godiva chocolate, he would buy her a chocolate bar, claiming that at least it had chocolate in the center unlike the boxes that had syrupy fillings. Now that is romantic: they loved each other and did not judge. I think their acceptance of idiosyncrasies made for a strong, long marriage.

31 You have to be emotionally healthy to meet someone emotionally healthy. That's one thing I've gleaned from my psychotherapy work, at least. And that's why delaying having children can, for many people, be a very empowering option. For some women, the ticking biological clock can exert so much pressure to settle down that they do so before they're ready, and sometimes with someone who is the wrong match.

32 More than ever, men are doing the nurturing along with women. My research and personal experience strongly indicates that children who have fathers who are nurturers and mothers who work outside the home are the most confident. This traditional role reversal is also better in that it helps the man to not only know and appreciate his family more but to live a healthier and longer lifestyle, as well as have his wife take some of the financial responsibility off of him, which validates her sense of importance as an individual.

33 Double standards are eroding. In my mother's time, women used to bury their own career goals to bolster their husbands' goals. My husband, in contrast, sometimes drives me into the city for my television appearances when he could be working himself, and the fact that we are both supporting one another in our careers has been positive for our family.

Putting Myself First While Also Being There For Others

For years and years, I struggled with the desire to take care of others while also doing justice to my own personal ambitions. Since turning sixty I have really internalized something I suspected all along. In order to take care of other people, we have to first take care of ourselves. That way, we can be happy for other people, rather than jealous. We can be good partners without getting resentful when we feel our needs are being pushed aside. We can draw boundaries to protect our feelings, even when people seem to be asking for time and energy commitments that are impossible to give.

34 Control the driver's seat. Once, when I was driving, my husband leaned over from the passenger side and took control of the wheel. *Bam*—we got into an accident. I guess that moment was symbolic of our life where he felt he had to take over or care of me. Do not let anyone take over; never give your power away, to anyone.

35 Stay away from people who try to steal your thunder. The people in your life who are mean, angry, or demanding are not worth your time. My advice at sixty-nine? Don't try to fix people. Either a person is a friend to you, or they are not.

36 If you are happy, don't let anyone tell you you're not. Isn't it annoying when men yell "smile" at women as they're walking down the street? In the same vein, I do not like to be told that I seem unhappy, when really I am just thinking things over or perhaps am acting less peppy than usual. We should not have to walk around acting effervescent 24/7. In the past, I was sensitive to being told that I did not seem happy, when really I felt happy. I worried about the message I was projecting, rather than being confident about what I was feeling inside.

Those days are gone. Now, if anyone tells me I seem unhappy, I take it with a grain of salt and am thankful that I know I feel, and need no one's approval of my happiness.

37 Take care of yourself. Here's what I wish I could tell my younger self, and what I will definitely keep telling my children (regardless of their age): learn to hold your own personal ambitions close to your heart even when you are caught up in the whirlwind of other people's wants and needs.

Breathing New Life Into Our Careers

I have noticed that people older than sixty are breathing new life into their careers. They are invigorated and empowered to make their mark. Retiring and sitting on the beach in Florida holds less and less appeal. I am certainly not tempted by it these days. My personal experience with breathing new life into my own career after sixty came with some lessons.

38 Say yes. I had long been drawn to the idea of having a voice in the media -- so when I received a call from publicists Ryan and Mark based on my LinkedIn page, I was ready and agreed right away. My first experience in a television studio, giving advice about family issues, felt like having surgery: agonizing, painful, and wrenching to the point there I wondered why the hell I was putting myself through this.

Shortly before I got that call, I had gone to see a psychic. She said this was my "lucky year" and advised me to trust whatever opportunities came my way. I believed her. Sure enough, a slew of syndicated television and radio shows followed that first agonizing appearance. I was branded as Dr. Frieda and gave advice on current events as well as all kinds of family issues.

39 The first time will be a mess. My first radio show, for instance, was a disaster. Right before I was supposed to call in to the station, the doorbell rang. It was the babysitter and I could not open the door. Her mother was calling and beeping me on the cell phone and on the line I was using. The dog was barking and the parrot was screaming. How I got through that show I'll never know. I do know the babysitter's mother said she will never work for me again. (The second time was better.)

40 Speak loudly. Despite the agony of that first television appearance, I felt great afterward. I started doing more and more appearances, and my confidence grew. I felt like my voice was getting stronger and the sense of reaching more and more people across the country was really satisfying.

41 . . . And keep speaking, even when you're crying. Before the media appearances started, I had been doing some public speaking at my synagogue because I wanted to tell my father's story. The first time I spoke, I had just been told some bad news about my mother's health. But I was so determined to tell the story that even though I was crying about the news, I went on to finish it. It felt good to share something when I felt on the verge of loss myself. I'm glad I kept speaking, loudly, even as my voice was wavering.

42 Being "productive" isn't about money. When I did all that research on marriage and happiness early in my career, as I described earlier in this book, I found women who had given up their own career goals for marriage generally reported feeling "empty" and experienced loss of identity. After sixty I learned that the more productive I was, the more fulfilled I felt—regardless of how much money I had.

Whenever anyone asks me what I am doing I always say, "keeping busy." Sometimes I do not feel like justifying how I spend my time, and I do not like when people look over my shoulder. I am not looking to be judged. When I'm productive and busy, it's for myself and no one else. It's taken me over sixty years to internalize this lesson, and I am still working on it.

43 Accept your professional style. Working under a deadline works for me. I'd known this about myself all my life, but it really came to a head when I started appearing in the media after sixty. I was often told to research topics with only a tiny sliver of time, and I embraced my tendency to thrive under this kind of pressure. My advice: if you know your working style, do not try to be something you are not. Try to find ways to work that fit your style, especially after the age of sixty.

44 Chaos is inevitable. When I into television studios to make appearances, I do not like to leave my family at home. So often the kids, my husband, and I pile into one car, sometimes at a moment's notice. It can be chaotic and sometimes my family has to drop everything, but I feel stronger with their support.

Once, I was calling in to a radio show from home and somehow the host misconstrued something I said about slavery. Just when I was going to defend my statement, our parrot started screaming and then one of my psychotherapy patients called. Annoyed at the chaos in my home, the radio host angrily asked, "Did someone just buzz you on your phone!?" When I said yes, he hung up. He never took my calls again, and I never got to explain my misconstrued comment. At first I was annoyed by the whole thing, but then I realized that chaos is a part of life. Life can be inconvenient, and it is frustrating to be misunderstood, but it is not the end of the world.

45 Relinquish vanity (sometimes). Once when I was en route to a television studio in the City, probably with Josh, Jaret, Ari, and Ken in the car with me, I found out that there would be no one available at the studio to do my hair and makeup. Because I had been expecting someone to be there, I went on without any makeup at all, and when I watched the tapes I saw blemishes I didn't even know were there. However, like so many other things, after sixty I am able to let this moment of vanity go. After all, there will be other appearances.

46 You can "do it all" in a day. One day, very recently, I had seven radio interviews for Fox News from seven to eleven in the morning. I timed it so I could run upstairs at six forty-five, wake up Ari for high school, and then at my next break at seven fifteen I would get the twins ready for school. So I spent that morning running upstairs to wake

up kids, and then running downstairs to pretend everything was calm. On the phone with Fox I talked about
psychopaths, Trump, and anything else they asked me to
comment on. I then had two phone sessions with psychotherapy clients before calling in to a radio show to discuss
being a sore loser. Then it was time to deal with cranky
people: I appeased a neighbor who demanded to know
why I wasn't calling her back in time. And before I knew
it the kids were home and starving.

Knowing that I was taking care of the people around
me while also doing something for myself made my voice
bolder on the phone, and my thoughts clearer. It was a
nonstop day and I felt strong. I like days like this, even at
sixty-nine.

47 Be ready for last-minute opportunities. Once when I
was sitting in my car I was called for a show. I sprang into
action: I got on the bus and had my daughter carry out
some last-minute online research for the interview while
I was on the way to the City. When I arrived at the studio,
there was more chaos: I did not even know which building to go into. But according to people at the TV station,
that was one of my best performances. Recently, when I
went to a local town hall meeting, people were still talking
about it, which made me smile. It would have been easy,
after all, to say no and stay in my car.

Once, staff from a television station asked me to pre-
pare to discuss the Black Lives Matter movement. I prepared for hours. When I arrived, they greeted me with,
"Are you ready to talk about Korea?" Gulp. I said yes

right away and winged it. At this point, I have gotten so sure of myself that when television stations ask whether I am ready to discuss certain topics that were never even mentioned before, I say absolutely. And somehow, with this confidence, I seem to pull it off. If you find yourself in a similar unexpected situation, have faith and try winging it: you may find yourself flying along, and will be glad you had faith in your abilities to adapt and wing it.

48 Laugh at naysayers. Every time I would share my media ambitions with my father, he used to say, "Don't go on TV; you won't know what to say." Other people have laughed at my ambitions, at many different stages in my life . . . but after the age of sixty, after going through pregnancy and motherhood at that unbelievable age, I feel empowered to laugh right back. Laughing off criticism that has gotten me far. I wish I'd had such thick skin earlier in life.

49 Proceed boldly. I used to worry about people not taking me seriously. As we know, many people, and especially women, feel this way throughout their lives: they worry that they will exposed as a "fraud," regardless of how much they have accomplished. But after sixty, I let go of that fear of being mocked. After all, I took a lot of flack for giving birth at sixty, so it could not get much worse! Now, I not only brush the fear of not being taken seriously aside, but I also proceed boldly. We all should. This attitude works. Based on these television appearances, I have been offered a possible show, a one-woman act, a performance on PBS about my research, a movie, and a reality show. I am interested in learning more about all of these opportunities, except for the reality show.

I love being in the media. When I was younger, I would never have imagined that in my sixties I would finally be doing what I always wanted to do. I love having the answers and most of all I love that people are actually listening. If there's something you have always loved, it is never, ever too late to jump right in.

Whatever your age, I hope you proceed boldly too. Never be afraid to be dynamic, someone with a passion and feelings—someone who is vulnerable, someone who is strong. Just be everything you are and take the risk of being rejected. It is worth it.

50 A wrinkle is not an illness. Women today have set such high standards that they can't keep up with their so-called needs. A wrinkle will set them back as if they have some illness.

Feeling Confident and Vital

In my sixties, I feel more vital than ever. I am not falling apart yet. I represent who I am, not who I am supposed to be, with the way I dress and wear my hair and no, I dont look like I am trying to be something I am not. I look natural and not out of place. I am just who I am on the outside as I am on the inside. I am not afraid not to fit in to what society says I should be.

Women often fear becoming "invisible" as they get older. I had these thoughts when I was younger.

But as it turns out, I did not have to fear getting older. Am I invisible? Not exactly. Over the hill? No way: I am on top of the hill. For people who ask whether I'm retiring, I ask, "Retiring from what?" Don't put me in a box so you can feel comfortable; I no longer need your approval. And if you don't like it, then you don't like me—and that is ok.

European women, from what I've seen, know just how to flirt and have relationships with men of all ages. They do not try to hide every wrinkle. I think that stems from confidence and feeling sexual, which far better than trying to look younger forever. Unfortunately, Americans stigmatize aging more than our counterparts around the world do. Don't internalize that stigma.

51 Healthy is sexy. A woman's curves are feminine; let's see more of that. Skinny is for runway models. Even they are setting different standards. Marilyn Monroe was famously a size twelve. She was sexy and every bit a woman. Just ask any man.

52 Don't be afraid of years passing. With each passing year, I feel better than ever. Every decade of my life I feel that my turn is over, just to feel and look better. Go figure. We should never fear getting older; fear itself will keep you from living your life.

53 Every decade seems old till you go on to the next one.
If you're reading this in, say, your thirties and wish you could go back ten years, know that in your forties you may romanticize your thirties in exactly the same way. Perspective is everything.

54 Take celebrity advice with a grain of salt. It always bothers me when a movie star such as Christie Brinkley who obviously had plastic surgery tells us about her face cream, as if to imply that if you take it, you will look like her. Yeah, give me a beauty budget of a hundred thousand dollars and I will have a hairstylist, makeup artist, plastic surgeon, dermatologist, and personal trainer and then maybe I can also look like that. Don't get me wrong; I am not bitter. I love that she is proud of being over sixty and beautiful. But we need to be honest with ourselves and know that buying celebrities' products will not make us look remotely like them.

55 Nothing is more attractive than feeling invigorated.
So many people over sixty are shedding the old versions of themselves for brand new versions. Who you are today has a lot to do with who you used to be. If you were interesting, fun, lovable, and caring, you will continue to be that same person. I would rather be with someone with character than a younger version of me who did not know which way to go or who I was, or was waiting for someone to give me permission to be who I wanted to be.

56 Confidence, after all, is beautiful. Confidence is not walking into a room with your nose in the air and thinking you are better than everyone else; it's walking into a room and not having to compare yourself to anyone else in the first place.

The Authority Is You

As a new mother the first time around, I worried about what other people thought of me. Remember those other mothers that gave me weird looks in the elevator as I went off to school, despite having young children? They seemed to spend every waking moment catering to their children and raising the perfect family. Looking back, it is possible that I was projecting my own anxieties onto these other mothers, who I perceived to be so very judgmental. In one television interview, they quoted me saying that as you get older you learn that "the authority is you." I am proud to have said that, and with every passing year I learn new ways to stand behind that statement.

57 Unlike Internet critics, real-life people are supportive. When I first had the twins, I was treated like a local celebrity. When we went to a town barbecue soon after the "birth heard 'round the world," for instance, someone rushed up to carry our folding chairs for us, which really was far from necessarily. In my community, I felt people's eyes on me in a friendly way. People walked by me and smiled; I sensed that sometimes they did not want to approach me, feeling I might want to be alone after the media hype. They were polite and respectful.

Sometimes women came up to me when I was shopping to offer their congratulations. I received gifts from people I did not know. The temple sent me ready-made meals for the holiday. From media outlets, I received T-shirts and flowers with requests to appear on their shows. I had to get a new answering machine because the calls were constantly coming. People that lived in other countries would somehow find my phone number. At school, I was recognized as the woman who had twins and who spoke on TV about family and news issues. Even though I was called "grannymom," no one asked (to my face, anyway) whether I was the twins' grandmother.

58 Don't keep up with the Joneses. One Halloween I noticed that my neighbor across the street had decorated his home. So I set out to do the same: I bought pumpkins, straw, and signs and spent hours putting them up until I felt I was finished. Then I looked across the street and saw that the decorations I first saw were the tip of the iceberg: he was putting up all kinds of gadgets and mannequins. I decided not to try to copy his decorations, but just to enjoy them from afar.

59 If you have children, don't waste energy on impressing their teachers or classmates. That's something I learned in my sixties, anyway. These days I do not like to compare my children to their friends. Growing up, one of my sons

did not like sports, but I pressured him into playing baseball. I regret that. He is excellent with computers, and I
wish I had encouraged him to pursue this early on rather
than trying to get him to participate in activities he didn't
really like. I pushed him into baseball because I felt competitive with the parents of other, more athletic boys in
his class—a common issue, and one that we should not
inflict onto our kids.

Parents are competing for grades more than children,
or at least it seems like that in my area. I do not worry
so much about the twins' grades, at this point. Instead, I
try to give them hands-on experiences in their free time,
to bring about a lust for learning that comes from within
which will last well beyond their school years (hope-
fully).

60 Perfect houses don't contain perfect people. You know
those huge, grandiose homes you sometimes see? If you
were to walk through any of these lavish front doors, you
would not see perfect families with pure happiness all
around. No matter how much money people make, they
all have issues: relationship conflicts, hard decisions about
household expenses, childcare problems. Regardless of
whether you are a billionaire or a person of modest means,
life can bring illness, divorce, drug abuse, alcoholism—the
list goes on. In my sixties, I have made some progress in
not assuming other people's lives are charmed while mine
is hard.

With each year, I feel less concerned with keeping up
with the Joneses and more convinced that I am the only

real authority on my own life and happiness. I'm not saying this secure sense of peace kicks in automatically on your sixtieth birthday; I'm just saying that I get better about it as each day passes. And that's something to look forward to.

I may have been the oldest person to give birth to twins in the United States, but I am of course not the first person in history to experience a profound sense of re-invigoration when society was telling me to slow down and sit quietly in the background. Whatever your age, and whatever challenges may be making you feel less than capable, I hope that my experience will drive home one truth: no matter who (or how old) we are, we are living every day for the very first time. At any given moment, it is absolutely possible to start something fresh and empowering. It is never, ever too late to feel brand new.

FURTHER READING

The following books shed light on aging, fertility options, and more.

Bach, Richard and Russell Munson (photographer). *Jonathan Livingston Seagull: The Complete Edition.* New York: Scribner Reissue Edition, 2014.

Birnbaum, Frieda. *What Price Power: An In-Depth Study of the Professional Woman in a Relationship.* Infinity Publishing, 2006.

Brinkley, Christie. *Timeless Beauty: Over 100 Tips, Secrets, and Shortcuts to Looking Great.* New York: Grand Central Life & Style, 2015.

Charlesworth, Liza. *The Couple's Guide to In Vitro Fertilization: Everything You Need to Know to Maximize Your Chances of Success.* Boston: Da Capo Press, 2004.

Cruikshank, Margaret. *Learning to Be Old: Gender, Culture, and Aging,* Third Edition. New York: Rowman & Littlefield Publishers, 2013.

Fonda, Jane. *Prime Time: Love, Health, Sex, Fitness, Friendship, Spirit—Making the Most of All of Your Life.* New York: Random House Trade Paperbacks, 2012.

Gullette, Margaret Morganroth. *Agewise: Fighting the New Ageism in America.* Chicago: University of Chicago Press, 2011.

Hammarberg, Karin. *IVF and Beyond for Dummies.* Hoboken, New Jersey: For Dummies, 2011.

Matthews, Rebecca. *IVF: A Patient's Guide.* Lulu.com, 2011.

Moody, Harry R. and Jennifer R. Sasser. *Aging: Concepts and Controversies,* Eighth Edition. New York: SAGE Publications Inc., 2014.

Northrup, Christiane. *Goddesses Never Age: The Secret Prescription for Radiance, Vitality, and Well-Being.* New York: Hay House, Inc,, 2015.

Richmond, Lewis. *Aging as a Spiritual Practice: A Contemplative Guide to Growing Older and Wiser.* New York: Avery Reprint Edition, 2012.

Rubin, Lillian. *60 On Up: The Truth About Aging in the Twenty-First Century,* paperback edition. Boston: Beacon Press, 2008.

Sandberg, Sheryl. *Lean In: Women, Work, and the Will to Lead.* New York: Knopf, 2013.

Van Dyke, Dick. *Keep Moving, and Other Tips and Truths about Aging.* New York: Weinstein Books, 2015.

Wallner, Alexandra. *Susan B. Anthony.* New York: Holiday House, 2012.

Weber, Robert L. and Carol Orsborn. *The Spirituality of Age: A Seeker's Guide to Growing Older.* South Paris, Maine: Park Street Press, 2015.

Weschler, Toni. *Taking Charge of Your Fertility: The Definitive Guide to Natural Birth Control, Pregnancy Achievement, and Reproductive Health,* Revised and Updated Edition. New York: William Morrow Paperbacks, 2015.

ACKNOWLEDGMENTS

Thank you to my children, Alana, Jaeson, Ari, Jaret, and Josh, for all the wonderful experiences I have had with you so far. Special thanks to Alana for reaching out and helping me with ideas that are creative and supportive.

Thank you to my husband Kenny for supporting my pursuit of truth and meaning.

Thank you to my editor, Erica Gordon-Mallin, for her input and excitement about the book.

Finally, thank you to all of my supporters.